LONG TIME COMING

THE GUY'S GUIDE TO EXTENDING ORGASM FOR FULFILLING SEX

VICTOR GOLD

Copyright © 2020 by Victor Gold.

All Rights Reserved.

No part of this publication may be reproduced, distributed, or transmitted in any form or by any means, including photocopying, recording, or other electronic or mechanical methods, or by any information storage and retrieval system without the prior written permission of the publisher, except in the case of very brief quotations embodied in critical reviews and certain other noncommercial uses permitted by copyright law.

ISBN: 978-1-63161-077-6

Published by TCK Publishing
www.TCKpublishing.com

Get discounts and special deals on our best-selling books at
www.TCKpublishing.com/bookdeals

Sign up for Victor Gold's newsletter at
www.victorgold.net/free

DISCLAIMER

Though this book is written by a heterosexual man, it is inclusive and its principles apply to lesbians, bisexuals, gays, transgender people, and queers. Many of the ideas in this book flow from the tantric traditions and the tantric ideal is represented by Shiva, the male aspect of creation, and Shakti, the female aspect of creation. However, the sexual techniques described in this book work for everyone if correctly applied. The truth is everyone is responsible for their own orgasms regardless of their sexual orientation, and anyone can learn to properly direct sexual energy

Please consult with your partner (if you have one) and get their consent before attempting any of the sexual techniques mentioned in this book. Awesome sex invariably contributes to good health and a more joyful and fulfilling life. May this book help you connect with yourself and your sexuality at a deeper level than you've ever known.

To the Mother and Father of All That Is,
and to Aimée, my most vivid reflection
of the sacred feminine.

TABLE OF CONTENTS

PREFACE	2
INTRODUCTION	4
THE SEXUAL POTENCY PRINCIPLES	9
CHAPTER 1: SEXUAL SECRETS OF THE FAR EAST	11
CHAPTER 2: A TRANSCENDENT SEXUAL EXPERIENCE	23
CHAPTER 3: WOMEN ARE SEXUALLY STRONGER THAN MEN	27
CHAPTER 4: THE DIFFERENCE BETWEEN EJACULATION AND ORGASM	32
CHAPTER 5: MALE EJACULATION FREQUENCY MUST BE REGULATED	46
CHAPTER 6: G-SPOT MASSAGE	49
CHAPTER 7: FEMALE EJACULATION	60
CHAPTER 8: HOW TO AVOID MALE EJACULATION	66
CHAPTER 9: SEXUAL LOVE: THE HEART-GENITAL CONNECTION	77
CHAPTER 10: FEMALE SEXUAL SATISFACTION IS VERY IMPORTANT FOR MEN	83
CHAPTER 11: THE CHAKRA SYSTEM	87
CHAPTER 12: USING BREATH CONTROL TO AVOID MALE EJACULATION	96
CHAPTER 13: THE FEMININE VERSION OF SEX: SOFT STYLE	106
CHAPTER 14: FINAL THOUGHTS	112
BIBLIOGRAPHY	117
ABOUT THE AUTHOR	124

PREFACE

This book is intended to revolutionize your sex life and inspire you to rethink your sexual behavior. Here you will learn the art of ecstatic lovemaking, and in the process, you will learn to prolong your sexual orgasm for a half-hour, an hour, or more. Though it may seem counterintuitive at first, prolonging your orgasm will depend on your ability to avoid a conventional genital release. Contrary to what you've been led to believe, your highest goal in sex should not be to come, but rather to cultivate the necessary restraint to hover indefinitely in the tiny, ecstatic space just before climax. As you will soon see, that is your *highest* option in sex. This little-known sexual secret—foregoing the urge to come in favor of something greater and more profound—is the key to attaining the extraordinary state of sexual ecstasy.

But before I get ahead of myself, let me start from the beginning. In 1981, I had the good fortune to attend a workshop entitled "Sexual Secrets of the Far East." It was there that I became acquainted with the ten sexual potency principles that I will share with you in this book. The impact these principles have had on my life has been immense. They were the catalyst for transforming my sexual behavior, healing my sexual relationship, and even illuminating my spiritual life—and they can do the same for you.

The sexual potency principles have been taught in the "mystery schools" of the Far East for roughly six thousand years, but until recently, they remained relatively unknown in the West. Mystery schools were created as secret societies, formed to prevent outside interference as initiates attempted to bridge the gap between the material and the spiritual worlds.

Though I was skeptical of the potency principles' relevance at first, upon deeper reflection, I came to understand why these esoteric rules have withstood the test of time. Taken together, the potency principles provide the foundation for a magnificent "new" sexual paradigm. Ultimately, I became so inspired by their coherent guidelines for prolonging orgasm and cultivating sexual energy that it wasn't long before I became an inspired student, and subsequently a dedicated sexual healer, tantra teacher, and orgasm coach.

Now it's your turn to study and apply these same sexual potency principles. Once you master the basic techniques, you can begin to explore the transformational power of extended orgasm and the expanded states of consciousness that inevitably follow.

Your life is about to change.

INTRODUCTION

I can say with near-certainty that very few of you have received proper training in sexual matters. How do I know this? Well, there are only a handful of credible people on this planet teaching the mysteries of the sexual arts. You don't learn this stuff in high school, college, or even medical school. In fact, I'm not aware of any school in America that teaches the art of ecstatic sex. So, it's not surprising that the majority of people reading this are unschooled in this important subject. As you will soon see, much of what you think you know about sex has come from extremely questionable sources. Even something as basic as the sexual urge is widely and grossly misunderstood.

Men in particular have been burdened with several erroneous assumptions regarding sexual behavior. These misguided beliefs have not only curtailed access to the spiritual dimension of sex, but they've also contributed to low sexual vitality, poor self-esteem, relationship difficulties, and a lack of respect and understanding between men and women. Collectively, we men have been misled by parents, teachers, religious leaders, friends, untrained lovers, pornography, and even the sexual marketplace. These dubious sources are not to be trusted! But unfortunately, too many of us still believe the bullshit we were taught.

As a consequence, if you are a guy, you have been saddled with several destructive and limiting beliefs about sex that have become a part of your subconscious operating system. These beliefs infest your sex life like flesh-eating parasites: back in the 1960s, modern sex researchers William H. Masters and Virginia E. Johnson, after observing hundreds of couples having sexual intercourse in their laboratories, felt obliged to call the American bedroom, "a national disaster area." As you will see, not much has changed since then.

SAD NEWS FOR AMERICANS

In a sex survey conducted by *The San Francisco Examiner* in 1999 (the most comprehensive since the 1948 Kinsey Report), researchers reported that more than 40 percent of the women and 30 percent of the men surveyed had no interest in sex, could not orgasm, or suffered some other sexual dysfunction. The list of problems plaguing the American sexual experience included lack of sexual desire, physical pain during intercourse, inability to become sexually aroused or to complete sexual acts, premature climax, and anxiety about sexual performance.

THE LIMITS OF WESTERN SEXOLOGY

My point is this: if you don't have the sex life you desire—if your sexual experience isn't filled with ecstasy, bliss, wonder, and awe—then you're being shortchanged when it comes to a very important part in "The School of Life." If that's the case, your subconscious mind—with its outmoded, outdated beliefs about sex—must be reprogrammed, and that is the spirit in which this book was written.

If your sexual education comes from conventional Western sexology, then this book constitutes a major paradigm shift. It offers a broader perspective that includes both an energetic and spiritual context for your lovemaking. Western sexology is generally devoid of energetic considerations and spiritual wisdom: a grave omission. The failure to acknowledge the inherent unity of sex and spirit, misplaced focus on male ejaculation, and utter ignorance of extended orgasm's transformational power are some of the foremost limiting factors of modern sexology.

ANCIENT WISDOM

Over the course of many centuries, the ancient cultures of India and China developed a comprehensive body of wisdom concerning the creative uses of sexual energy. As they explored the deeper aspects of their sexual nature, these ancient cultures discovered a gateway to spiritual enlightenment through the practice of cultivating and transforming sexual energy. At some point, it became clear to them that the line dividing sex and spirit is extremely thin—if it exists at all. Modern investigators concur, since virtually every major study on spirituality includes sex, and virtually every major study on sex includes some aspect of spirituality.

The classical erotic practices of Hindu tantra and Chinese Taoism were designed to be equal parts art, science, and spirituality. It was intended that these sexual practices evoke mystical, transcendent, non-ordinary states of mind. Both tantra and Taoism operate on the principle that sexual intercourse, when correctly understood, can harness the creative power inherent in the sexual force and use it for true spiritual mastery. These ancient traditions offer you the chance to use the vehicle of conscious sex to elevate all aspects of your life.

These ancient practices, when mastered, will enable you to transform sexual (orgasmic) energy into spiritual illumination by prolonging and heightening the journey of arousal without genital release. Why no genital release? Well, as far as men are concerned, release is actually a negative phenomenon. Simply put: men lose vital energy each time they come. The little-known sexual secret of foregoing your explosive genital orgasm in favor of something more profound is the key to multiple male orgasms. Prolonging orgasm will ultimately lead you to the first essential in living the spiritual life: "unity consciousness," or oneness. This is the miraculous experience of merging with all of existence and gaining knowledge of the divinity within.

A NEW SEXUAL PARADIGM FOR MEN

In the current Western sexual paradigm, male sexual power is strongly linked with a rock-hard, throbbing erection. Failure to attain one in a timely manner is considered dysfunctional and inadequate. In the Eastern sexual paradigm, however, a man's ability to direct internal energy, whether or not his penis is erect, is the real measure of sexual power. In other words, "sexual potency" is really "energy mastery," since this is what offers the greater sexual reward.

Similarly, the conservation of semen—in contrast to the "cum shot" lauded by modern pornography—is the true hallmark of potency in the new sexual paradigm. Considering potency in this way may seem strange to you at first, but as you begin to implement these principles in your sexual life, you will discover a deeper sexual power that is based first and foremost on transforming orgasmic energy into expanded spiritual awareness.

AN EVOLUTIONARY LEAP IN CONSCIOUSNESS

My hope is that this book will help men and the women who love them to explore the merits of conscious sexual practices. The transformational power of extended orgasm has an important role to play in the evolution of our species and the perfection of our culture. My goal is to demystify tantric lovemaking, and I want you to be able to integrate these enlightened sexual practices into your own life, should you choose to do so.

Be aware that the metaphysical implications of a truly cosmic sexual experience are profoundly inspiring. Should you be lucky enough to experience it, the blessings of transcendent sex will surely expand your consciousness and provide you with a broader spiritual perspective. On a practical level, it will leave you relaxed, at ease, at home, energized, and blissfully uplifted. For perhaps the first time, you will feel natural in sex. You will become transformed so that sexual pleasure is a true source of ecstasy. At the very least, my aim in writing this book is to reduce the gap between what you would like your sexual experience to be and what it actually is.

LIFE FORCE AND SEXUAL ENERGY ARE VIRTUALLY THE SAME

Before I continue, let's define energy as I use it in this book so we're all on the same page. Energy has been called by different names throughout the ages. In Hindu tantra, it is known as "prana." The Chinese call it "chi." In America, it is most commonly called life force energy. It's important to understand that by any name, life force energy is virtually the same substance as sexual energy. In fact, sexual energy represents the life force in your body. What does this mean? It means that the hornier you are, the stronger your life force. The stronger your life force, the stronger your sexual urges are apt to be. Modern sexology completely misses this important point.

If the concept of energy is new to you, you may be wondering why you've never been aware of it before now. After all, it has always been a huge part of your life. The answer is simple: the influence of energy in your life is so subtle that it's nearly impossible to perceive without proper training.

EVERYTHING EXISTS AS ENERGY

Energy follows a self-perpetuating cycle so natural and imperceptible that unless you specifically bring your awareness to it, you hardly ever notice it. Energy becomes virtually indistinguishable from all of the physical sensations that you are accustomed to experiencing. Though mystics and scientists alike tell us that everything exists as energy, most people don't realize that this includes not only your thoughts and feelings, but also (seemingly) empty space.

If you are skeptical about the concept of invisible energy, you're probably someone who requires physical evidence before you accept something as real. But, if you consider that the difference between a corpse and a living human being is based solely on the ability to breathe in unseen air—well, I'm sure you get the picture. When it comes to the existence of energy, let the truth be known! Whether you acknowledge it or not, we all live in the realm of energy.

THE SEXUAL POTENCY PRINCIPLES

1. Women are sexually stronger than men.
2. Ejaculation and orgasm are not one and the same.
3. Ejaculation is not necessary to complete a sexual exchange.
4. Male ejaculation is not the most ecstatic moment in sex.
5. The frequency of male ejaculation needs to be regulated.
6. Female sexual satisfaction is of the utmost importance to men and women.
7. Dynamic sex must involve both the heart and the genitals.
8. Recycled semen is a rejuvenating source of energy.
9. The condition of the sex muscles determines the degree of sexual pleasure.
10. The way you breathe determines the duration and quality of your sexual experience.

CHAPTER 1

SEXUAL SECRETS OF THE FAR EAST

During a trip to my local health food store many years ago, I happened to glance at the community bulletin board. A flyer promoting a workshop entitled "Sexual Secrets of the Far East" caught my eye. Here was an opportunity to learn about ancient Hindu tantric and Taoist lovemaking techniques. In light of a lifetime of fascination with sexual pleasure, that was more than enough to stimulate my imagination and arouse my interest. I had heard a little bit about tantra from friends who had referred to it as the "yoga of sex," but in those days, I was totally ignorant about the sexology of these ancient cultures.

I had practiced the stretching postures and breathing techniques of yoga off and on for years. I valued the flexibility, strength, and meditative perspective I'd gained, but as far as I knew, yoga bore no connection with sexual intercourse. If you yourself practice yoga, you may have noticed that most yoga teachers rarely, if ever, speak of its sexual applications. Later, after years of scholarly effort, I came to understand that many yoga postures are actually lovemaking positions intended to prevent an unwanted male ejaculation and to facilitate the upward movement of sexual energy in the body.

Who knew?

A TURNING POINT

I became excited about learning sexual secrets from the other half of the world, so I decided to attend the workshop, though at the time, I had no idea what a turning point in my life this opportunity would prove to be. It was there that I was introduced to the ancient wisdom that I will share with you in this book.

What I learned at the workshop gave me the foundation for a new sexual approach. Although these sexual potency principles are roughly six thousand years old, they were new to me at the time. Even today, these sexual secrets still aren't widely known here in the West, and at first glance, many of these ancient concepts sound outlandish. To say that I was skeptical would be an understatement. I found the new information so compelling, but I needed to take a closer look.

NON-EJACULATORY SEX

One principle that was difficult to digest stated that it was not necessary for a man to ejaculate to complete a sexual exchange. Like most men, I found this idea ridiculous at first—even a bit masochistic. For a man to have sex without seeking a climax just seemed wrong. Wasn't having the most explosive climax the whole point of great sex? Yet Charles, the workshop facilitator, spent a great deal of time reciting the benefits of ejaculation control and the virtues of seminal retention. He was quite convincing as he shared his own experiences and reinforced them with the wisdom of ancient tantric masters.

Charles became my mentor. He opened my eyes to the exciting possibilities of non-ejaculatory sex. Of course, I knew that adopting the practice of seminal retention would be challenging. It would require both a major shift in my core belief that coming was my highest option in sex, and a radical change in my sexual behavior. In addition, it was clear that if I was serious about making the leap to non-ejaculatory sex, I would certainly have to improve my ejaculation control skills—and at the time, I really had no idea what that would look like.

THE PHYSICAL SKILLS CAN BE ACQUIRED

I learned that the physical skills needed to master the ejaculation process could be acquired in several weeks by performing a daily regimen of "sexercises" designed to strengthen the muscles used in sex. When properly toned and activated, the sex muscles can prolong intercourse by preventing unwanted male ejaculation. The additional time not only helps build arousal to higher peaks for both partners, but it also gives the woman, whose erotic response requires more time to build, the chance to finally fulfill her orgasmic potential. Furthermore,

Charles explained that developing the sex muscles offered men the key to multiple orgasms without ejaculating.

Now I was really intrigued, even though I had no idea how I could ever hope to accomplish such a remarkable feat.

Initially, I was uncertain if I could make the physical and mental adjustments necessary for non-ejaculatory sex, but by the end of the workshop I was highly motivated to achieve mastery. With my teacher's encouragement, and faced with the possibility of becoming a true sexual dynamo, I was eager to learn and grow.

Though I listened intently to every word Charles said in the workshop, I paid particular attention to the theory of male ejaculation control. He made it abundantly clear that the ability to avoid an unwanted ejaculation separates the men from the boys. Tantric sages went even further. They considered the avoidance of genital release a central point in elevating sex from the animal level to the spiritual. As the words sank in, I realized that the concept of elevating sex to a spiritual level really appealed to me, but once again I had no idea how this could be accomplished. I learned that avoiding ejaculation was intended to reconcile female sexual satisfaction with male well-being. Not only does this prolong the act of intercourse, but by retaining his semen, a man prevents the energy drain that is so prevalent in ordinary sex. Until then, I had never imagined that the sleepiness I felt after climax was actually a sign of energy loss.

It soon became clear that all the great traditions of sacred sexuality are concerned with cultivating higher consciousness—meaning, a man who can generate copious amounts of sexual energy and who has the lovemaking skills to successfully contain the energy of orgasm in his body has a huge spiritual advantage. By doing so, he can initiate the alchemical process of transforming orgasmic energy into spiritual enlightenment by directing the intense sensation of pleasure upward. In doing so, the orgasmic energy nourishes the heart and ultimately reaches the brain, where the spiritual faculties reside and where consciousness is transformed.

THE GAME PLAN: UP NOT OUT

In ordinary sex, when men come, the vital sperm energy shoots out from the tip of the penis. Except for the purpose of procreation, this needless output of energy is utterly wasteful. After all, the fluids of procreation carry the most powerful and condensed creative energy available—yet the conventional male sexual experience is totally devoted to expelling that precious life force out of the body.

In contrast, tantric and Taoist sexual practices contain the orgasm(s) inside the body and direct ecstatic energy upward. In this scenario, the spine is viewed as an energy pathway through which orgasmic energy can be propelled upward, away from the genitals. Raising sexual energy diffuses the buildup of pressure in the balls and genitals, which compels untrained men to come. Now I was beginning to understand why a healthy, strong, flexible spine was such a major focus in my yoga classes.

POTENT SPERM ENERGY NOURISHES THE BODY

In esoteric sex, the energy of arousal is awakened in the area between the legs just like ordinary sex. But according to Taoist physicians, with no ejaculation forthcoming, the semen is contained in the body, where it can be rerouted and ultimately reabsorbed. Keeping the vibrating energy field of millions of living sperm inside the body is a game-changer. The tantric masters believed that the potent sperm energy nourishes organs, tissues, nerves, and glands. The upward movement of orgasmic energy (raising the seed) not only invigorates the heart, but activates previously dormant brain cells, ultimately expanding the mind and accelerating the process of awakening.

A DAUNTING TASK

It dawned on me that raising sexual energy accomplishes what drugs like LSD are reputed to do—expand human consciousness—but without all the negative side effects of synthetic drugs. Though I no longer use them, my previous experimentation with psychedelics (as a child of the sixties) made me quite familiar with the benefits and negative side effects. I had experienced both bad trips and illuminating ones, but to think that consciously directing orgasmic energy upward could be as profoundly awakening as an acid trip shocked me. I was especially curious as to how a man directs sexual energy upward. I wondered if I could ever learn to do it. I'd learned the practice of channeling energy through my hands at massage school, but channeling sexual energy through my penis seemed like a daunting task.

From my own independent study, I knew that the pioneering sexual researchers Masters and Johnson considered ejaculation control to be an important part of lovemaking. They recommended repeated interruptions in the sex act as a way of prolonging intercourse, in the hope that men could gradually learn to control their ejaculation as a first step toward satisfying women. But their work never included anything about the energetics of sex, nor did they concern themselves with spiritual considerations. Apparently, those expanded concepts were as foreign to them as they were to me.

WORTH THE EFFORT

Those of us at the workshop were cautioned that the more turned-on we get, and the higher the level of arousal we attain, the greater the temptation is to release the buildup of sexual excitement in the form of an explosive genital discharge. For this reason, seminal retention is regarded as a truly delicate art to be mastered. It requires great attention to every detail as the journey of arousal unfolds and inevitably escalates.

Charles insisted that learning to control ejaculation is well worth the effort—especially since the explosive genital discharge has so many shortcomings. "If you're really honest with yourself," he suggested, "you might admit that coming seldom feels deeply fulfilling, and it tends to short-circuit the intimate connection with your partner."

A light bulb flashed on in my brain. For the first time, an expert in the field of human sexuality was helping me connect the dots. I was stunned! Could habitual energy loss from coming so much be a factor in my seemingly endless array of relationship difficulties? Was that the reason I'd had so much difficulty maintaining an intimate connection with my partner? Of course, I knew that successful relating depends on the interplay of many factors, but the notion that I could be sabotaging my intimate connection with women in this way was nothing short of a revelation.

THE DEVASTATING POST-EJACULATION LETDOWN

To emphasize this point, one of the workshop attendees read a quote from Jolan Chang, the author of *The Tao of Love and Sex*. Jolan's words seemed to be addressing me personally:

"Nearly every man has experienced the devastating aftereffect of ejaculation, the sudden feeling that he has lost nearly all interest in his woman, which may even lead him to wonder why he has ever loved her. Intuitively, most women quickly notice that their lover has become remote and indifferent."

THE ANSWER TO MY PRAYERS

As Charles revealed the benefits of seminal retention, I quickly became convinced that *this* could be the answer to my prayers. I had heard previously that having non-ejaculatory sex was unhealthy. Now I was learning the opposite: that seminal retention contributes to the maintenance of a youthful, vigorous, healthy body with high energy levels, clarity of mind, and increased sexual potency. In fact, the ancient tantric masters considered seminal retention to be the foundation of penile strength. They thought of semen as a man's greatest treasure, worthy of conservation. I was beginning to suspect that my previous beliefs were nothing more than unfounded malarkey.

PREPARING TO WIN

When the workshop ended, I couldn't wait to begin training. Actually, I practiced all the way home in my car. Believe it or not, we were taught "sexercises" (see Chapter 8) that could be performed in our cars while stopped at red lights. Being athletically inclined, I understood that practicing was really just preparing to win. In my mind's eye, I saw that my next sexual encounter would give me the opportunity to demonstrate my newly practiced skills. I strongly felt that my success as a lover would ultimately be determined by the quality of my practice sessions. At this point, I was a man on a mission.

Men, if you'd like to increase your libido and firm up your erections, by all means stay sexually active, but stop ejaculating for a few weeks and take note of what happens. Many men with difficulties achieving or maintaining erections are merely coming too often. Their batteries are run down and need to be recharged. Listen to what your body is saying. No man, no matter how strong he may be, can ejaculate excessively without feeling like he's lost a piece of himself. My own experience tells me that coming too often initiates a downward spiral that feels a bit too much like impotence and decay.

PRESERVING YOUTH-GENERATING HORMONES

Preserving semen, on the other hand, translates into greater staying power. Tantric masters have always claimed that during arousal, the activated sex glands release powerful, youth-generating hormones that nourish the body and increase vitality. To heighten these benefits, why not stop wasting your hormone-rich semen? Though it's become common knowledge in Western culture that there is a strong link between harmonious sexual activity and the retardation of aging, Taoist physicians believed that when the sex glands are stimulated and semen is retained in the body, the health benefits are amplified.

SEXUAL DESIRE REMAINS AT A FEVER PITCH

The benefits of seminal retention are huge. You can have sex more often for extended periods and stop and resume as often as you like. By containing ecstatic energy, you stop short-circuiting the arousal process. You may experience sensations of erotic intensity, excitement, and intimacy unlike anything you've ever felt in your life. Working together with a partner with the intention of preventing—or at least *delaying*—ejaculation until the optimum moment for release tends to keep sexual desire at a fever pitch.

AVOID THE FLATTENING OF SEXUAL DESIRE

Men, if you choose to forego ejaculation, you'll avoid the flattening of sexual desire that is so prevalent after coming. After all, the post-ejaculation crash has been a source of unhappiness for men and women since the dawn of time. Consider that most men experience sexual pleasure only *until* they ejaculate. Thereafter, they enter a time of mourning: a refractory period during which the penis does not respond to additional stimulation. In fact, after coming, your penis may even *hurt* if touched. Even that would be bearable if it weren't accompanied by a post-coitus letdown that tends to sabotage the close emotional bond that sexual intercourse induces, the same bond that many women find so appealing.

ACHIEVING AN ALTERED STATE OF CONSCIOUSNESS

Charles said that I could experience multiple orgasms by hovering close to the point of climax for an extended period, but without coming. By doing so, I would inevitably achieve an altered state of consciousness. An altered state is an inner experience where perceptual reality shifts, the doorway to the mystical realms opens, and the depth of connection with your partner deepens. Achieving an altered state can be a profound experience: it may not last, but it will not easily be forgotten, either.

By successfully employing the retention of semen during a period of heightened arousal, communication with your partner becomes sweeter and more loving. As sexual energy expands into the heart area, a heart-opening process is apt to take place that awakens a man's nurturing, feminine qualities. If you're anything like me, under these conditions you'll naturally reveal more of your gentle and affectionate side. The upward movement of orgasmic energy into the heart inevitably enhances your ability to give and receive love. And don't be surprised if your "heart-on" includes a tendency toward vulnerability, emotional expression, and honesty—always a big turn-on for women.

When a man contains his sexual excitement, he can satisfy his partner more thoroughly, guiding her through not one but *several* intense orgasms. Now her feminine energy can open to your masculine energy more fully. In return, you are sure to receive not only love and affection, but also the thrilling excitement of a lusty and passionate partner. Those marvelous electric feelings of arousal, desire, aliveness, heightened sensitivity, and ecstatic pleasure can now be experienced on a regular basis.

CREATIVE SELF-PLEASURING

Armed with the new information about seminal retention, my post-workshop evenings were spent pleasuring myself—but in a completely new way. Charles recommended that I practice what he called "creative self-pleasuring." For the first time in my life, I would seek peak arousal *without* attempting to climax. In so doing, I was constantly left in a joyful, horny state. Previously, I had always felt that arousal demanded release—with a partner, if I had one, or by literally taking matters into my own hands.

Now, things were different. I let go of the old ways that no longer served me. Charles predicted I would find semen retention to be so incredibly powerful that my relationships with the women in my life would be forever transformed. He suggested that as I began to cultivate sexual energy, my personal power would heighten and my self-confidence would soar.

Charles hated the term "masturbation" because the derivation of the word reflects an anti-pleasure attitude. It essentially means "to abuse oneself"—a devious sex-negative message right there in the word's root. He recommended that I substitute the term "self-pleasuring." I'm sure you'll agree that *self-pleasuring* is a much more uplifting idea, and certainly more accurate to what you intend to accomplish. Let's face reality! Human beings are sexual beings. Pleasuring yourself is entirely natural, yet masturbation is still considered taboo by some sex-negative people. I prefer comedian Woody Allen's advice: "Don't knock masturbation; it's sex with somebody I love."

THE DOWNSIDE TO SELF-PLEASURING

If there is a downside to self-pleasuring, it's this: virtually all men do it purely to ejaculate. According to the tantric sages—and my own personal experience—losing semen through self-pleasuring is more energetically harmful than losing it through intercourse. After all, the energy loss through self-pleasuring has no inflowing feminine energy to compensate. Also, many men develop the habit of coming too soon. They learn through intense, regular practice how to get off quickly and efficiently. Pretty soon, they are performing unconscious, habitual, robotic movements that tend to curtail sexual creativity and spontaneity, especially when they have a partner.

Unfortunately, many men place so much emphasis on the shortsighted goal of ejaculation that they fail to develop an appreciation for the subtle feelings of arousal that would continue to grow in joyful intensity, far exceeding a paltry ejaculation, if only they would prevent their release.

MY GAME PLAN

My self-pleasuring game plan was as follows: stimulate myself to erection and maintain my erection without coming for thirty minutes. During that period of time, I was encouraged to bring myself close to climax a half-dozen times without shooting my load—a tall order, especially for a novice.

Each time I approached the point of no return, I was instructed to hold back my release in very specific ways. Of course, when you are attempting to avoid coming, it is just common sense to cease further stimulation at the appropriate time, often simply by removing your hand from your genitals. Obviously, it's better to be too early rather than too late. It's also helpful to consciously relax your anus and your genitals since unconscious tension in that area tends to induce ejaculation. Expanded breathing from both the belly and the chest is helpful since it tends to calm the central nervous system, and that inhibits your urge to ejaculate. Lastly, be still! Movement is too stimulating if you are on the cutting-edge of a release.

Once the orgasmic energy is safely contained, my mentor instructed me to direct my awareness to the middle of the chest in order to redirect the energy of arousal there. This strategy of using your awareness for redirecting sexual energy upward is based on a cosmic law that states that *energy follows awareness*. This is just another way of saying: *where the mind goes, the energy flows*. As a practical application of this energetic truth, I was able to successfully redirect the energy of arousal away from the source of pleasure (the genitals) and into the love center (the heart). So you see, the movement of sexual energy can be successfully directed to a specific target. I utilized all of these "holdback" techniques each time I approached climax.

CONTAINING THE ENERGY OF AROUSAL

Initially, it was quite challenging to learn to function in a relaxed manner in the midst of the accumulated sexual tension that my self-pleasuring generated. Mastery of this process requires an increase in body awareness, breath awareness, and energy awareness. It takes practice to focus your mind away from the source of your sexual pleasure, but it can be done! At times I felt like a 110-volt toaster suddenly hooked up with 220 volts—just smoking away! Although I was often tempted to climax out of habit, I was determined to refrain from coming for ten self-pleasuring sessions. I just had to find out if seminal retention was all it was cracked up to be.

Charles assured me that an accidental ejaculation or two in the midst of my training wasn't the end of the world. If I did ejaculate, I was instructed to enjoy the brief, intoxicating rush of pleasure, and monitor my sexual energy for the next twenty-four hours. The idea was to notice how the discharge had impacted my vital energy reserves. The results of my practice sessions were impressive: as the cultivation of sexual energy accumulated, I noticed a definite increase in my energy level. I required less sleep; my erections were firmer; I felt sexier, more confident and alive; and, on several occasions, I experienced true heightened awareness. And, unsurprisingly, when I did finally choose to come, the intensity of my discharge was *off the charts*.

A BIGGER BANG FOR MY BUCK

By the way: did you know that the intensity level of an ejaculation can actually be measured by how many involuntary contractions the prostate gland undergoes during the release of semen? All men are familiar with these delightful pumping sensations, which are experienced as spasms of pleasure.

From observing my own sexual apparatus during ejaculation, I noticed that eight involuntary contractions were normal for me. Men who are seriously depleted from over-indulging might experience as few as one puny spasm. On this particular occasion, after holding back through ten creative self-pleasuring sessions, I experienced twenty-one powerful contractions. My explosive discharge reflected the penile strength and sexual prowess I had gained in training.

From that moment forward, I was sold on the power of seminal retention. Subsequently, I became a master at avoiding ejaculation. Now, many years later, I can truly say that the teachings have withstood the test of time. My ability to generate, contain, and transform orgasmic energy still impacts my life. There's no doubt in my mind that I'm a more evolved person because of it.

CHAPTER 2

A TRANSCENDENT SEXUAL EXPERIENCE

Fast-forward one year after the workshop. While making love with my girlfriend, I had a full-fledged mystical experience—my first. As I mentioned previously, a truly enlightened experience may not last, but it cannot be easily forgotten. By this time, I had become quite masterful at non-ejaculatory sex. Through intense practice and the successful application of the potency principles, I had learned to savor and *extend* my orgasm(s) for maximum sexual pleasure.

On this occasion, however, I apparently outdid myself. This incident was special! It happened as a result of the prolonged buildup of peak orgasmic energy without a genital release. By exercising extreme caution and restraint, I was able to successfully hover on the cutting-edge of a genital discharge for an extended period. Call me the multi-orgasmic man, if you will. I was orgasmic for so long, and so blissed out, that I morphed into an extraordinary altered state of being. My physical body seemed to transform itself. It no longer felt like *matter*; I could no longer perceive my body as a material thing. My physical form dissolved into a tingling, vibrating, electric, unified energy field. It was no longer possible to discern where my body ended and my partner's body began. Our energy fields meshed. First mine with that of my partner, and then both with the greater universal energy field. Somehow, I had transcended physical reality and energetically merged with the universe. For the first time in my life, I experienced my own divinity; miraculously, God and I were one. There was no separation between us! By the grace of ecstatic sex, I had a direct experience of merging with the divine. I later learned that this heightened state was a known spiritual phenomenon called "unity consciousness."

MERGING WITH EXISTENCE

In that euphoric state, there was no time; no past or future, just total presence in the here and now. My breath stopped—yes, I actually stopped breathing! My mind was spacious, empty, and devoid of thought. I had risen *above* thought, resting in the ecstatic state of pure consciousness. It should be noted that Eastern philosophy recognizes that God is *within*. Now I was experiencing that for myself. And once I experienced the magnificence of that illuminating bliss, I was forever grounded in the reality that extended orgasm is one of the most accessible ways to directly experience the unity and interconnectedness of life. The realization that "all is one" had such a profound spiritual influence on me that it precipitated a thirty-five-year study of tantric sexual practices that ultimately led me to a career as a *tantra* teacher, a sexual healer, and an orgasm coach.

BRAIN RESEARCH

It is interesting to note that recent scientific research into the structure and operation of the human brain has subsequently provided me with valuable scientific insights as to what actually took place that day. We all know that the brain is divided into right and left hemispheres. But though the two sides of the brain were designed to work together like the two wheels of a bicycle, in virtually all people the two hemispheres are unbalanced with one side or the other being dominant. Scientists refer to this as *brain lateralization*. In this state, the brain filters and interprets reality, but only in *dualistic* terms like good and evil, up and down, here and there, me and not me, and so on. In this state, reality appears to be a multiplicity of separate things. Everything is separate, and worse yet, often in opposition to each other. You are separate from me and I am separate from God. Welcome to ordinary third dimensional reality!

MOST PEOPLE PERCEIVE THINGS IN DUALISTIC TERMS

When the brain is functioning in this type of "split-brained way," it's as if you are allowed to use only one wheel of your bicycle at a time. Imagine how less efficient it would be to ride your bicycle if you had to switch from one wheel to the other unable to use both at the same time. Unfortunately, for most people, this is exactly how the brain functions—you can effectively use only *one* side at a time. One side of the brain is always switched off. With this type of inadequate brain integration, you are predisposed to experience yourself as separate from the rest of the world. Though mystics and physicists agree that separation and duality is an illusion, they remain the hallmark of ordinary reality.

SOCIETAL PROGRAMMING REINFORCES DUALITY

Our societal programming reinforces duality by training you to seek one thing and avoid another, to move toward pleasure and away from pain, to do good and not bad, and so on. The mind dwells in the world of duality. Under these conditions, life takes on an isolated, guarded, "me-against-them," fear-based view of reality. This pattern tends to evoke a habitual flight-or-fight response. So how can the elegant feeling of unity, oneness, and interconnectedness that I experienced during my transcendent lovemaking be explained?

MEDITATORS OVERCOME BRAIN LATERALIZATION (DUALITY)

It turns out there are several ways to balance the two brain hemispheres. One way is through meditative practice whereby the meditator overcomes brain lateralization through some form of concentrated focusing. Whether it's following the movement of the breath, repeating a mantra, staring unblinkingly at the tip of a flame, or another chosen point of focus, the effect on the meditator's brain is the balancing of the two brain hemispheres. This enlightened state is known as *brain synchronization*: a condition in which both brain hemispheres produce strong brain waves of a single, coherent rhythm, also known as *whole-brain functioning*. This condition is associated with profound inner peace, happiness, intense creativity, and deep spiritual connection to all of existence. In this state the meditator experiences the *non-dual*, cosmic view of reality: whether you call it *oneness* or unity consciousness, it's the experience of merging with existence.

Once I uncovered the information on brain research, I immediately began connecting the dots. My sexual play provided me a strong point of focus. My ability to relax into peak sexual arousal for an extended period altered my brain activity. Orgasm provided a lift-off that propelled me into a state of brain synchronization (whole-brain functioning). With an increase in communication between both sides of my brain, I experienced an immediate end (temporary though it may be) to the sense of separation that I normally think of as ordinary reality, as well as the stressful feelings that often accompany it.

A SYNCHRONIZED BRAIN PERCEIVES UNITY

A synchronized brain is unlikely to see reality as "me against the world." Dualities become less pervasive and the unity and interrelationship of all things become apparent. With a balanced brain, you experience life as a connected whole. While any kind of meditative focusing will bring about some degree of brain synchronization, the greater the focus, the deeper the sense of connectedness and unity tends to be.

THE FOCUSING EFFECT HAPPENS NATURALLY DURING SEX

No wonder you feel so connected to your lover(s) just before and during sexual play (not necessarily after male ejaculation). Your intense sexual focus initiates changes in your brain. When orgasms are extended and internalized as they were during my mystical experience, whole-brain functioning is more apt to take place.

Unfortunately, due to the predominance of brain lateralization, the experience of unity and oneness remains just a fuzzy, intellectual concept for most people. If that's the case for you, your view of reality will tend to reinforce feelings of *separateness* along with the accompanying painful feelings of isolation, fear, anxiety, and stress.

However, all is not lost! As I've showed you, your ability to prolong orgasm is an *ecstatic* doorway into a more favorable and enlightened view of reality than you might now experience. From where I sit, brain synchronization is the product of extended orgasm. They are like two sides of the same coin. I'm no scientist, but it's not much of a reach for me to say that sexual ecstasy alters brain chemistry in a good way.

CHAPTER 3

WOMEN ARE SEXUALLY STRONGER THAN MEN

The idea that women possess greater sexual strength than men has always seemed very much in line with my own experience, but I realize that it's difficult for many men to accept this premise at face value. Whenever I bring up this point in my workshops, it's a given that several men will vigorously challenge me. I understand why: the male ego is a powerful force. It's in our nature to want to be recognized as the stronger sex. We see ourselves as bigger, stronger, and physically superior to women. Granted, in virtually any activity in which speed, size, and strength are paramount, men have an innate advantage. In a hypothetical wrestling match for control of the planet, the smart money would be on the fellas.

However, physical prowess is not the proper criterion for evaluating sexual strength.

"Sexual strength," as I call it, is the ability to generate and contain sexual excitement and ecstatic pleasure without terminating the orgasmic flow and without losing vital energy. It is properly measured by how successfully an individual manages his or her sexual energy. Ask yourself: After lovemaking, are you energized or fatigued? Are you happy, enlivened, and sexually fulfilled? Do you feel emotionally connected to your partner? Or are you fatigued, melancholy, disconnected, empty, and emotionally withdrawn?

WOMEN HAVE THE ADVANTAGE IN THE BEDROOM

Sorry guys, but it's the truth. Sexual strength is one area where women possess a clear advantage. Think about it: a woman can sexually receive a man (or many men) for as long as she pleases. When she is open, receptive, and properly aroused, a woman's sexual appetite can seem inexhaustible. As the arousal process unfolds, she becomes energized, awakened, and increasingly engaged. In the sexual arena, women have *two* clear biological advantages over men. First, they don't have to maintain an erection to have sex.

Second, and more to the point, *women do not lose vital energy through sex.*

In Erica Jong's 1973 book *Fear of Flying*, she alludes to the sexual strength of women:

"The female has a wonderful all-weather cunt. Neither storm nor sleet nor dark of night could faze it. It was always there, always ready. Quite terrifying when you think about it. No wonder men hated women. No wonder they invented the myth of female inadequacy."

COMING OR GOING?

A man's sexual appetite is more easily fatigued. No matter how lusty he may be, by carelessly spilling his seed virtually every time he becomes aroused, the resultant energy loss may compromise his sexual strength. Nearly every man has at one time or another experienced the humiliation of sporting an unfashionably limp penis at an inappropriate moment. In fact, a drooping, unresponsive phallus symbolizes the sexual imbalance between men and women. When a man comes, his sexual energy goes. With his discharge, he loses his erectile capacity and his sexual appetite. Worse yet, his ability to stay emotionally connected to his partner may diminish as well. If he comes too often, the experience may leave him exhausted, drained, and ready for sleep. In their post-ejaculation stupor, some men even get dressed and physically leave their partner. Have you ever heard of a woman doing this? Erica Jong again offers a liberated woman's perspective:

"What could be more poignant than a liberated woman eye-to-eye with a limp prick? All history's greatest issues paled by comparison with these two quintessential objects: the eternal woman and the eternal limp prick."

At heart, most men are as daunted by a woman's seemingly infinite sexual capacity as they are fascinated by it. Unfortunately, a woman's sexual power also makes some men feel insecure. Too often these men feel the need to compensate with some other strength. I ask you: Could sexual insecurity be the primary reason that men have sought physical, political, financial, intellectual, and religious advantage over women throughout all of history? Could that be, as Erica Jong theorized, why they created the myth of female inadequacy?

MEN MUST SHARPEN THEIR BEDROOM SKILLS

Rather than getting defensive, I encourage men to sharpen their bedroom skills to match women's innate sexual advantages. In this way, both sexes benefit. What women come by naturally, men can achieve with practice. Conscious sexual techniques are designed primarily for men in an attempt to achieve sexual equality with women. Conscious men must learn to conserve sexual energy, delay its release, raise it into the higher energy centers, and let the ecstatic energy propel them to higher states of consciousness.

A woman is sexually stronger than a man because she *needs* to be, biologically. Her body must bear the strain of producing and nurturing children. Women have other advantages, too. Their orgasms occur in a different part of the brain, are deeper, longer, and can be repeated over and over. Women are less focused on their genitals during sexual exchanges: their tendency is to expand and open to altered states of consciousness, out-of-body experiences, mystical union with their partner, and the deepest states of meditation. All the bedroom skills men spend years attempting to master with their special techniques are naturally available to women by nature of their physiology.

WATER AND FIRE

In comparing the relative sexual strength of men and women, Chinese sexology likens them to fire and water. Fire belongs to men: they are more volatile, active, and swift. Women, like water, are more placid: their movements are calmer, and no matter how hot fire may be, water can always extinguish it.

Women have an altogether different arousal cycle than men. I recently heard a radio ad promoting a male herbal potency formula. It maintained that women take four times as long to climax as men. I'm not sure about the accuracy of the math, but any attentive man knows that women do tend to heat up slowly and cool down slowly, just like water. Men may be fast, but they tend to burn themselves out. Women have endurance.

GOOD NEWS FOR MEN

The good news for men is that equality, at least on the level of sexual performance, can be attained in spite of a woman's innate sexual advantages. Men merely have to learn how to substitute orgasm for ejaculation (more on that later). By doing so, male and female energies are correctly balanced and one can transform the other. Continuous fire in the form of prolonged sexual intercourse will provide the time that a woman needs for her water-like energies to boil. Fire and water in balance produce steam. Steam rises—just like the ascent of orgasmic energy rising up into the heart and brain during conscious sexual union.

TEMPERING THE MALE SEXUAL NATURE

Men who are sincerely interested in upgrading their lovemaking skills must learn patience and control. By tempering their quick and volatile sexual nature, both men and women benefit. Men can learn to slow down and still maintain their passion. In fact, slowing down will invariably *increase* arousal, since it gives the escalating sexual buildup a chance to intensify and expand. On the other hand, it isn't really possible for women to speed up and get ready sooner. You can't force the issue. If you want the teakettle to boil, you must apply heat and wait.

A SLOW HAND

Most women appreciate a lover who exhibits the so-called "slow hand." It affords them the time they need to build the arousal that intensifies sexual pleasure. Women find nurturing, playfulness, intimacy, and sensuality delightfully arousing. It also takes the focus off their genital area and, paradoxically, that is what turns on their genitals—or heats up their water. Unlike men, until they are highly aroused, women do not respond well to strong focus on the genitals. For many women, arousal can be achieved more easily by initially *avoiding* her genitals entirely and instead concentrating on awakening the rest of her body. As a general rule, her genitals should be the last thing touched, not the first.

YES, THERE ARE EXCEPTIONS

If a passionate, orgasmic woman makes love often, she tends to remain juicy. She may not require much foreplay to be ready. For example, my lover sometimes has erotic dreams when we sleep together. On such occasions, she is already turned-on, well lubricated, and ready for penetration. If that's the case, she will ask me to enter her "sacred space" without need of further stimulation. If I'm feeling openhearted and receptive, my normal bodily response is to become instantly aroused and, in general, I willingly oblige.

AWAKEN HER WHOLE BODY

But more often than not, non-genital erotic play is essential for a woman's sexual readiness. I've yet to be with a woman who didn't appreciate that I took the time to awaken her whole body before I approached her vagina. Many women particularly enjoy it when men pay lots of attention to their secondary erogenous zones by kissing, scratching, sucking, gently biting, blowing, or licking those areas. These include the ears, throat, lips, breasts, belly, and inner thighs, as well as the tertiary erogenous zones, like her palms, ankles, head, and feet. In fact, sensual awakening of this kind is what many women thirst for and what many women *require* before they warm up to genital play. But how many men actually take the time to awaken their lovers slowly—particularly when they've been with the same woman for a while? If you have taken the time to fully arouse a passionate woman, you know that it is well worth the effort. It's like unleashing a tornado.

The bottom line is this: in spite of a woman's terrifying sexual strength, with proper training, any man can withstand the sexual neediness of a highly aroused and horny woman. All that's needed is for him to cultivate the ability to substitute orgasm(s) for ejaculation. Once he's mastered this skill, he can experience multiple, full-body orgasms, and his sexual apparatus can stay up and running indefinitely. At that point, sexual equality in the bedroom has been reached, and male ejaculation becomes entirely superfluous.

CHAPTER 4

THE DIFFERENCE BETWEEN EJACULATION AND ORGASM

Until now, far too many men have made the erroneous assumption that ejaculation and orgasm are one and the same. This is unfortunate, yet understandable, since from their earliest sexual explorations, men have observed over and over that orgasm and ejaculation always happen together. What men *haven't* been told is that these are actually two distinct physical processes, and that separating one from the other can be very useful.

It is vital that both men and women understand the distinction. Male ejaculation is a local genital release, a negative phenomenon in which men lose vital energy. Orgasm is a totally different animal. Orgasm engulfs the body, mind, and spirit. By refraining from the discharge of accumulated sexual tension, men can learn to preserve vital energy by substituting orgasm for ejaculation. Once this skill is mastered, the habitual male sexual routine of ejaculating with every orgasm can be seen for what it is—sheer lunacy.

INITIAL SKEPTICISM

The idea that it was possible to achieve orgasm without ejaculating shocked me at first. I couldn't even imagine how such a thing could take place. How could it be possible to separate the two? As far as I was concerned, ejaculation and orgasm seemed inseparable. And this was no small sampling: I must have ejaculated thousands of times, and each time ejaculation and orgasm happened together! Even in traditional sexology, the words climax and orgasm are usually interchangeable, with no distinction drawn between them. Learning that they could be experienced separately was a belief-shattering concept.

My workshop notes reminded me that equating orgasm with ejaculation is a mistake that the ancient sages wisely averted. They hungered for the crescendo of orgasm, rather than the crash of ejaculation. They recognized that a man's orgasmic pleasures would only increase when he withheld his ejaculation. To the ancient sages, ejaculation was trivial. They understood that it was little more than a brief, intoxicating rush of pleasure. It could never be deeply fulfilling. How could it be? Men simply lose life force energy each time they ejaculate. In contrast, they knew orgasm to be a peak, full-body, physical, emotional, and energetic experience that could even have mystical overtones.

REICH, OSHO, AND GRISCOM ON ORGASM

Wilhelm Reich, the noted German psychologist, was one of the first Western practitioners to draw a sharp distinction between climax and orgasm. Like the ancient sages, Reich referred to climax as a predominantly genital and pelvic experience. On the other hand, he viewed orgasm as an experience in which the muscles of the entire body participate. Reich went on to say:

"Only through orgasm could we achieve a complete circuit of bioelectric flow through the body that is essential to mental and physical health. The complete flowing back of the excitation toward the whole body is what constitutes gratification. If you don't involve the whole body, said Reich, then you don't have a complete experience, and that dammed-up energy seeks outlets in other, often destructive, ways."

Twentieth-century tantric master Rajneesh, who later changed his name to Osho, describes orgasm as a purely energetic phenomenon:

"Orgasm is a state where your body is no longer felt as matter; it vibrates like energy, or electricity. It vibrates so deeply, from the very foundation, that you completely forget that it is a material thing. It becomes an electric phenomenon. You become a dancing energy vibrating."

Obviously, Osho's description of orgasm is not just a genital or even a whole bodily affair. It is a pure, energetic experience vastly superior to ordinary genital climax, but one that is seldom experienced in ordinary sex since ejaculation invariably short-circuits the process. Typically, before the expanding orgasmic energy has a chance to build to higher levels, and before it can circulate throughout the entire body, the energy is lost in the wasteful male discharge.

In her book, *Ecstasy Is a New Frequency,* Chris Griscom remarks:

"You can learn to experience sexual energy as pure energy in and of itself, which will lead you to what I call 'Cosmic Orgasm.' These are the higher realms of sexual experience that happen throughout the entire body, rather than just the genitals. People everywhere are beginning to experience these rare octaves of sexual potential and this will set in motion a new kind of sexuality that is based not on what you can extract from a partner, but rather the intensity of energy available to you, with or without a partner."

MY FIRST ORGASM WITHOUT EJACULATING

After digesting this new information, my initial skepticism gave way to fascination. I became highly motivated to embark on the training program my teacher proposed. I was assured that success required nothing more than the timely use of strong internal muscular contractions similar to the ones I already employ when squeezing out the last drop after urinating. Alternately squeezing and relaxing my sex muscles literally hundreds of times per day was the key to my success. Ultimately, my sex muscles grew so strong that I could easily prevent an unwanted ejaculation any time I wanted by squeezing my anal sphincter muscles at the appropriate time. And, by hovering close to the genital release point without coming, I could still experience the thrill of orgasm.

Sure enough, in just three weeks of daily practice, I succeeded in having my first orgasm without ejaculating. It felt like I was bearing witness to an extraordinary event, like the decoding of a mysterious and secret ancient teaching. These days, I regularly experience multiple orgasms without the conventional discharge that *ends* the fun, and I get the added benefit of not having to endure another depressing post-ejaculatory crash.

THE MYSTICAL ELEMENT

If you bring your awareness to the moment of orgasm, the borders of the "selfish" self fade, and the ego dissolves. The distinction between lovers may become so blurred that detachment of one from the other becomes impossible. The orgasm as a physiological process has such a profound psychological effect that it may provide access to a new dimension of spiritual awareness. It can raise the consciousness to super-heightened levels, where time and space are nonexistent and perceptual reality shifts beyond the normal three-dimensional physical plane. In other words, your orgasmic potential is much greater than you may have thought.

What I have been describing—namely, the difference between ejaculation and orgasm—are essentially two different types of orgasm. In one you empty yourself, in the other you fill yourself up. The genital orgasm is more common, but ultimately the less fulfilling orgasm. As I've previously mentioned, the genital release was the only kind of orgasm that noted sex pioneers Masters and Johnson were aware of. They defined it in the clinical context as "the sudden discharge of accumulated sexual tension resulting in rhythmic muscular contractions in the pelvic region characterized by an intense sensation of pleasure."

Virtually all men and many women are familiar with the explosive genital orgasm. Like Masters and Johnson, for a vast majority of sexually active people, the genital discharge is the only kind of orgasm that they have ever experienced. Though coming has been glorified in movies, books, magazines, television, and pornography, let's be aware that genital orgasms have a huge downside. They come with baggage (pun intended).

THE DOWNSIDE OF GENITAL RELEASE

By the very nature of its brevity, a genital release prevents a deeply fulfilling, memorable experience. I've already mentioned that it doesn't involve the entire body. It diminishes a man's erectile capacity and stifles his sexual desire. Many men even lose immediate interest in their partner, at least until their libido returns. In essence, it ends the fun. The party's over! It's like sticking a pin in a swollen balloon. Remember, men only experience sexual pleasure *until* they come, and the aftermath often includes an inconvenient post-ejaculation letdown. Perhaps most importantly, as far as the bigger picture is concerned, coming tends to eliminate the possibility of building enough ecstatic energy to access the mystical side of sex.

In his book *Love of the Two-Armed Form*, the enlightened spiritual master Bubba Free John describes the downside of the usual male genital release.

"The conventional orgasm is a genital discharge. It is a form of bodily elimination. It is sexuality lived after the model provided by the organs of digestion and elimination. It empties us. It is a form of reactivity or recoil. It separates us from others and from life."

Bubba Free John reinforces the notion that when men release sexual energy in a gigantic burst, they become temporarily exhausted. The result: reduced sexual tension, sexual desire, interest, and even consciousness. Sure, I've heard men say that coming is relaxing, but often a man may become so relaxed that he slips into unconsciousness. Yes, his discharge may be sleep-inducing (a sure sign of energy loss), but that's the extent of it. Think about it! How can a sexual exchange be deeply fulfilling if it diminishes a man's life force energy? It can't!

In *Taoist Secrets of Love: Cultivating Male Sexual Energy*, the author, Mantak Chia, offers a similar take on male ejaculation:

"Those who fully understand conventional ejaculatory sex know it grossly exploits every gland and organ. With ejaculation the internal pressure of life is expelled from the body, leaving behind in some sex-obsessed men only enough life force to fold the newspaper, squeeze food through the bowels and make for the psychiatrist's couch."

To sum up the master's advice on male ejaculation: there are two parts to sexual intercourse, the beginning and the end. *Remain in the beginning!*

IMPLOSIVE ORGASMS ARE FAR MORE MEMORABLE

Let me turn your attention now to the *monarch* of orgasms. This "higher" orgasm can be discovered only when the ordinary genital orgasm that so preoccupies most men is de-emphasized. This second type of orgasm is far more memorable and expansive than "shooting your load," but of course, it requires the avoidance of a genital release. It is commonly called an "implosive" orgasm. Implosive orgasms are comprised of multiple, almost-ejaculation *pleasure peaks* interspersed with blissful periods of relaxation known as "valley orgasms."

Implosive orgasms include the genitals but are *not* genital-focused. They engulf the entire body, mind, and spirit with ecstatic energy. Implosive orgasms are completely fulfilling. They permeate all the major energy centers including the heart (the love center), and the brain, where the spiritual faculties reside. Because implosive orgasms are kept *inside* the body, they allow you to benefit from the rejuvenating circuit that Mantak Chia calls the "animating current of life." This internal current travels to and invigorates every cell. An implosive orgasm is arguably the most intensely satisfying human experience. If you are lucky enough to experience them, you may find that implosive orgasms bring you closer to a state of religious awe, or what you may perceive as a *spiritual high*, than anything you are likely to experience in a church, synagogue, mosque, or temple.

IMPLOSIVE ORGASMS ARE SELDOM EXPERIENCED

Unfortunately, implosive orgasms are seldom experienced, since most sexually active men are still addicted to coming. Too many men still think that sex with a woman is the time to just jackhammer her like a piston until he comes. Sex for these untrained, insensitive men is always fast and hard. They are either unwilling or unable to slow down and soften their "macho" approach. Implosive orgasms require prolonged, leisurely, non-ejaculatory sex—something these men are almost incapable of conceiving.

IMPLOSIVE ORGASMS REQUIRE A GREATER SKILL SET

Now you know why accomplished male lovers seek to avoid genital climax! They've discovered something bigger and better. They have voluntarily surrendered their gushing genital climaxes in favor of a more controlled experience that, frankly, makes male ejaculation seem trivial by comparison. Yes, it's true that implosive orgasms require a greater skill set, especially for a man—but bedroom skills are an important attribute, don't you think? Ask yourself: How much time are you willing to put into learning to become a better lover? Let's remember, it is the untrained man who traditionally collapses his sexual apparatus with his habitual tendency to come. Avoiding climax will take your lovemaking abilities to the next level.

ECSTATIC SEX AND THE CONNECTION TO SPIRIT

Think of implosive orgasms as a vehicle into the mystical world of sex. As you will soon discover, there is a dynamic connection between sex and spirit, but not just any sex will do. To access the world of spirit, the sex must be *ecstatic*. In order for that to happen, the orgasmic energy must be contained and allowed to circulate throughout the entire body, which takes time, so the lovemaking must be prolonged. Containing and raising orgasmic energy can be learned with practice, but the starting point is to avoid coming. Learn to get to the point where you almost come, but hold back! Familiarize yourself with playing on the cutting-edge of genital release, but without spilling over. As you will see, the interval just before your climax would occur is where the sexual magic happens, provided you learn to hover in the tiny space between peak arousal and genital release.

And yes, it is worth the effort for every man (and woman) to learn, since implosive orgasms provide the lift-off that propels you into *spiritual sex*, and that is the chief aim of every tradition of sacred sexuality.

A CLIMAX ISN'T JUST A PEAK

Now I realize that many men recoil in horror when they first hear about non-ejaculatory sex. The prevailing fear is that they would be sacrificing sexual pleasure for some abstract spiritual benefit. Let me reassure you that nothing could be further from the truth. Experience has taught me that withholding my discharge *heightens* bodily pleasure to an extraordinary degree. The sexual pleasure that is available by avoiding climax goes beyond anything that the chronically ejaculating man gets to experience in sex. Accomplished male lovers—those who have mastered seminal retention—know that calling ejaculation the "climax of pleasure" tells only half the story. A climax isn't just a peak—it's an end as well.

THE TINY GAP WHERE ALL THE MAGIC HAPPENS

Most guys are as yet unaware that the most intensely pleasurable time in sex exists at the interval right before ejaculation would occur. I am referring to a tiny gap that lies precisely between peak arousal and genital release. With practice, this tiny space, when entered cautiously and with total awareness and restraint, can be savored and extended for maximum sexual pleasure. Learning to successfully navigate this ecstatic space without coming is a man's highest option in sex. Here skilled male lovers can experience what can best be described as a series of almost-ejaculation pleasure peaks and rejuvenating valley orgasms. These repeatable orgasms provide men with the opportunity to prolong the ecstatic feelings of orgasm almost indefinitely. Just as a woman is capable of multiple orgasms, men are capable of multiple, almost-ejaculation pleasure peaks and valley orgasms.

Of course, this tiny gap is virtually imperceptible to the untrained neophyte. These men typically get swept away with the heat and intensity of arousal, making their ejaculation inevitable. Even accomplished lovers are challenged to successfully hover on the cutting-edge of genital orgasm without coming. It's a bit like walking across a tightrope high above the ground without a safety net below. One accidental slip and it's over. An accomplished lover is like a master surfer successfully riding wave after blissful wave to shore. An untrained lover, on the other hand, is like the novice surfer that repeatedly gets wiped out.

TEAMWORK WITH A SENSITIVE PARTNER IS HUGE

For a man to successfully play on the cutting-edge of climax without coming may require teamwork with a sensitive partner. You see, a man invariably rides a woman's wave of arousal. This means that her mounting excitement tends to trigger his release. If he has mastered control of his ejaculation, her emerging passion need not be a problem. But if not, and she becomes so turned-on and so orgasmic that she loses control, it will inevitably take him *over* the edge.

To avoid this scenario, she must become aware that his rapid pelvic thrusting, his panting breath, and his increasingly loud moans and groans are red flags. They signal that his escalating excitement is growing too hot. This is the moment of peril! As a good teammate, she must immediately cease further stimulation. By responding to a pre-arranged signal from her partner, the couple becomes perfectly still. In stillness, they begin the process of relaxing and letting go. Together the lovers employ deep, synchronized breathing (see chapter 12) that diffuses the accumulated sexual tension away from the genitals, making male ejaculation far less likely. When relaxing and letting go is artfully done, he will lose about 30 percent of his erection. Once the threat of an unwanted ejaculation has passed, the couple may safely resume their preferred form of *pelvic expression*. This cycle may be repeated as much as needed. First you stimulate, then you delay! You are navigating the peaks and valleys of implosive orgasms. Of course, once he can pilot the ship alone, this kind of partner intervention will no longer be needed. At that point, she can lose control and orgasm to her heart's content. But until that time teamwork is essential.

THE TANTRIC WAVE OF BLISS

Successfully negotiating multiple pleasure peaks and blissful valleys without coming is known in tantric circles as "riding the wave of bliss." This is the methodology that leads to *sexual ecstasy*. Here's why! If you recall, I mentioned earlier that the interval right before a male climax would occur is the most intensely pleasurable time in sex. By hovering on the cutting-edge of climax, a man could theoretically savor and prolong his orgasmic pleasure almost indefinitely; and that is exactly what accomplished lovers do! That's what I have been trained to do, and that's what I encourage my tantric students to work towards.

Now, let's assume that the intensity level of an explosive genital release is 100 percent. You've reached a high state of arousal and the pressure between your legs is building; you can no longer contain the escalating excitement, so you climax. Let's compare that scenario with a guy who successfully hovers just below the genital release point without coming. Admittedly, this provides a slightly lower level of orgasmic intensity. The orgasmic intensity level drops slightly to 98 percent or 99 percent, but the difference is imperceptible. You are in the state of peak arousal. You are orgasmic, but you are not coming! The slight difference in orgasmic intensity becomes absolutely irrelevant, since a skilled male lover can have a dozen or more orgasmic pleasure peaks and valleys. Mind you, the pleasure peaks are actual orgasms that can be repeated again and again. The valleys are opportunities to retreat slightly by resting in stillness until it's safe to move again. Valleys are also orgasmic, and they require no effort. You simply rest and recover. And by the way, this strategy works equally well for women who prefer the ecstasy of prolonged, multiple, full-body orgasms, rather than the less fulfilling, brief, intoxicating rush of coming.

PLEASE DO THE MATH

So, the question then becomes: What would you rather experience in your sexual play? You can have one gigantic release of 100 percent intensity that may last six or seven seconds, or you can experience a dozen (or more) orgasmic pleasure peaks of 98 percent intensity, interspersed with periods of rejuvenating stillness (valley orgasms) that may last a half-hour, an hour, or more. Do the math! A dozen orgasmic pleasure peaks at 98 percent intensity adds up to 1176 percent worth of ecstatic pleasure. A lone climax of 100 percent intensity obviously cannot compare. I rest my case!

PREMATURE EJACULATION IS PROBLEMATIC

This type of extended orgasmic activity is potentially transformational. It can propel you into an altered state of expanded awareness. Prolonging the sexual dance is particularly great for the woman who requires more time before she can become orgasmic. When women are not given the opportunity to become fully aroused (usually due to an untimely male genital release), they can quickly become dissatisfied with their male lovers. If he has already shot his load before she can fully arrive, well, it's not a pretty picture. Many women seem to agree that perhaps the worst outcome in a sexual situation is to have a man ejaculate at an inappropriate time without considering if the timing is right for her. If this becomes their normal pattern of interaction, her resentment will likely grow into chronic hostility, avoidance, or withholding of sex. And why not, if she feels she's being used as nothing more than a sperm receptacle.

Sadly, sexual frustration is all too common. The unpleasant scenario of an untimely male release is the crux of sexual incompatibility between male and female lovers. Even if a woman does not blame her male partner, she may blame herself. Or, she may simply shut down reasoning that sexual relationships are just not worth the psychic toll and sexual frustration that she must endure.

MANY WOMEN ARE AS CLUELESS AS MEN

Interestingly, some women help to perpetuate unconscious male sexual behavior. They apparently have bought into the myth that even if they don't climax, their male partner should. Some women will do everything in their power, whatever it takes—intercourse, manual stimulation, fellatio, even faking orgasm—to induce a male climax. A woman may think she is doing her man a favor, but if she is constantly pushing him over the edge, she may unknowingly be eroding his sexual vitality.

A woman may feel that a man's discharge brings a sense of completion. It signals that he is done. It also lets her off the hook if she wants to get the encounter over with as quickly as possible. Some women don't know how to deal with a man if he doesn't come. Like many men, they too are programmed for his release. Somehow, they believe his discharge really matters. To these women, his discharge is a necessity. She may feel that she is more of a woman if she can make her male partner come. Subconsciously, a woman may think that something is wrong with her if a man doesn't come. Let me be perfectly clear on this point: a woman need not feel inadequate, offended, or upset if her male lover withholds his release. Chances are, it has nothing to do with whether she has pleased him or turned him on. The physical body has an innate wisdom. Sometimes the body may just say no! Sometimes the energy for sex is just not there! Intelligent people listen to their bodies. There is no good reason to ever force the issue. Force is the opposite of love.

FIREWORKS ALL NIGHT LONG

I've also come across some women who say that a big part of their satisfaction is derived from a man coming inside them. I encourage these women to try a different approach. They might find that they prefer it. Wouldn't you appreciate a skilled lover who can provide constant attention, endless pleasure and fireworks all night long rather than a guy who rolls over and goes to sleep after he has fired off his only "bottle rocket?"

POST-EJACULATION SYNDROME

At this point, I want to make you aware of a destructive pattern I've named *post-ejaculation syndrome*, since it describes how relationships suffer in the aftermath of male genital release. We've all heard how women hate it when men roll over and go to sleep as soon as they are finished with sex, but few people ever mention that the loss of energy from male ejaculation is the culprit. While many women want to experience the afterglow of lovemaking by staying physically and emotionally connected to their male partner, very often the intimate connection they seek is short-circuited so abruptly by his untimely discharge that it must seem to her that he turned off the television while she was still watching the movie. And rest assured many unpleasant altercations between sexual partners stem from harboring bad feelings about what happens, or doesn't happen, during and after sexual expression.

WOMEN SUFFER AS MUCH AS MEN

Though loss of energy after climax is predominantly a male phenomenon, women may suffer the consequences as much as men. After all, they are also part of the uncomfortable aftermath. Snoring after sex may just be the tip of the iceberg. This is such a profound realization that I want to emphasize this point: the degree of erotic play, interest, and emotional connection a man feels for his sexual partner largely correlates with the amount of sexual energy available to him. To put it another way: sexual depletion from excessive semen loss may sabotage a man's ability to feel loved, to act loving, and to appear lovable.

While some men have more stamina than others, most will experience at least some of the effects of post-ejaculation syndrome when they ejaculate beyond the frequency that is biologically comfortable. Post-ejaculation, a man's mood may go flat like an open can of soda; a noticeable but subtle change that colors his overall behavior. However, for some men, the emotional consequences are more extreme: loss of sexual desire, emotional withdrawal, irritability, moodiness, and indifference are fairly common. Ladies, does that remind you of anyone you know?

A PRIMITIVE GENETIC AGENDA

There was a time in my own life—before I was able to connect the dots—when *I* was a chronic victim of post-ejaculation syndrome. As I look back, it's all too clear that I was totally ignorant about the energetics of sex. Admittedly, there was an element of incessant striving and sexual greed in my lovemaking. My cultural conditioning kept reinforcing the notion that in spite of its brevity, ejaculation was the end-all, be-all goal. Too often, I would overindulge in sex to the point of seminal exhaustion. My sexual exploits were characterized by obsession and gluttony. The harder I tried to grab sexual pleasure, the more elusive it became. The more I spilled my seed, the emptier I felt. I became a victim of my own lust.

With each sexual exchange, I witnessed myself furiously racing toward another unfulfilling release. Too often, the loss of my precious sexual fluids went well beyond my body's comfort zone. Foolishly, I ignored the little voice in my head warning me that if I didn't moderate my excesses, it would only be a matter of time before I found myself in trouble.

GRUMPY AND REMOTE

When I found myself sexually spent, I would withdraw like a turtle into its shell. Predictably, my lover thought she had done something wrong. Regrettably, I would reinforce her insecurities by getting defensive and lashing out when she attempted to find out why I was so emotionally withdrawn. The drama that ensued could get so unpleasant that there were times when I questioned why I ever got involved with women in the first place. And this was a time in my life when I was living with a woman whom I treasured and adored.

Unfortunately, my sense of sexual depletion could be so devastating that my heart felt closed, devoid of love, emotionally shut down. Seminal depletion is destructive. It's depressing! On many occasions, it transformed me from a virile, powerful, and loving man to an indifferent, irritable, grumpy jerk—without ever knowing why.

PUTTING MY RELATIONSHIP AT RISK

By exceeding the boundaries of my biological limitations, I was repeatedly and unknowingly putting my relationship at risk. Yet due to the deeply ingrained, habitual, and *unconscious* nature of my sexual behavior pattern, neither my lover nor I understood the underlying cause of the problem. It's hard for me to believe now, but back then we were clueless as to why our relationship was so troubled. We were caught in a seemingly endless cycle of fucking, fighting, and forgiving each other—a destructive pattern, as I'm sure you'll agree.

Unfortunately, there aren't many positive role models in the area of healthy sexual behavior. Isn't it strange that there aren't any schools that teach proper lovemaking? It's such an important part of life, yet there is virtually no opportunity to receive formal instruction. That being the case, I guess it's not too surprising that my sexual behavior reflected a litany of mistaken beliefs and inappropriate behavior.

HORMONE FLUCTUATIONS INFLUENCE YOUR BEHAVIOR

In some ways, post-ejaculation syndrome is similar to a bad case of the premenstrual syndrome that some women experience. Both syndromes involve mood swings that result from hormonal changes. But in my opinion, post-ejaculation syndrome can wreak even more havoc, since it can occur again and again, at any time of the month, and its true nature remains a dark mystery to most people.

THE BATTLE OF THE SEXES

Could it be that a major obstacle to male/female harmony is the male addiction to ejaculation, and the resultant energy loss that precipitates post-ejaculation syndrome? At the very least, it contributes to the basic lack of understanding between men and women. In addition, its role in domestic drama, confusion, and emotional turmoil is still largely unknown.

Happily, the solution for men is as easy as mastering the art of seminal retention, since that is what invariably *transforms* the sexual dynamic between lovers. It offers men the chance to *cultivate* sexual energy instead of squandering it. The cultivation of orgasmic energy might be the single most significant change a man could make in transforming his bodily health and the health of his sexual relationship.

CHAPTER 5

MALE EJACULATION FREQUENCY MUST BE REGULATED

By now, you may be wondering if you should *ever* ejaculate—and if you do, when and how often. Taoist physicians teach that when a man's semen reserves are low, his health suffers. Semen was always considered a vital essence, a precious treasure not to be wasted. It was viewed as the most powerful and important source of male energy. Taoist sages considered one drop of semen the vital power equivalent of a hundred drops of blood.

No wonder men who squander semen feel like their batteries are run down! If these ancient physicians are correct, every seminal discharge is a bit like donating blood. Scientific analysis has shown semen to be a storehouse of nutrients far more valuable than any nutritional supplement you may presently take. And that's no exaggeration when you consider the life-giving and life-sustaining properties it possesses. I am referring to the copious amounts of human life force energy thought to be present in semen. I'd say this is a fairly important consideration since life force energy is what separates the living from the dead.

Most people are unaware that scientists have found creating sperm is a much greater priority for the body than previously imagined. It demands a diversion of resources that might otherwise go into assuring a man's long-term health. Taoist physicians have always claimed that as part of the body's deeply embedded genetic pattern for survival of the species, its first response after ejaculating is to direct all available energy to restoring the body's ability for procreation. Amazing as it sounds, sperm production seems to be given a higher priority than healing the body from illness or injury.

This premise might explain why some athletes choose to refrain from sex before important competitions. They recognize that the loss of energy from semen depletion could be a severe competitive handicap as the body strains to keep producing sperm. If ejaculating is a sometimes thing, it may not be significant. However, if it develops into a habitual pattern, as it does for many men, then over time it could severely compromise a man's health and sexual vitality. This brings up the question: Could sexual energy depletion be the untold reason that most men do not live as long as women? After all, most men continue ejaculating their whole lives—right up until death.

I know from experience that once I began regulating the frequency of my ejaculations, I grew more confident and felt stronger and more empowered. My emotions stabilized, and even my self-esteem improved. It felt like an uplifting, mood-enhancing drug, but without the negative side effects. By avoiding the trap of semen depletion, the relationship with my lover improved radically. In my case, avoiding genital release was a great example of the old saying, "An ounce of prevention is worth a pound of cure."

YOUNGER AND HEALTHIER MEN MAY EJACULATE MORE OFTEN

While the choice of whether or not to ejaculate is best left to the individual, it's important for men to understand the road map to energy cultivation. It begins when you realize that semen is a manly resource of vital energy that can be conserved and internally redirected to the rest of his body. To ensure greater sexual vitality, the frequency of male ejaculation should be based on a man's age and his level of health and fitness. Other considerations, such as heredity, stress level, and lifestyle also play a big part. It's just common sense that younger and healthier men may safely ejaculate more often than older, health-challenged men.

FIND YOUR IDEAL EJACULATION FREQUENCY

The challenge for every man is to find his own ideal ejaculation frequency. Let common sense prevail: if you have to work particularly hard one week, or if you're under a great deal of stress, you may want to come less often, or not at all. If you are relaxing on vacation and you feel healthy and strong, it may be no problem for you to ejaculate whenever you feel like it. The best advice is to know yourself. One thing is certain: for trained male lovers, coming is always a conscious choice, rather than an involuntary reflex. Most importantly, consider whether the timing is right for your partner. Remember that in conscious sex, a man's top priority is being in service to his lover.

For optimum vitality, you have to monitor your body's energy reserves to determine the proper timing and frequency for ejaculation. If you come and feel tired and it takes you awhile to recover your libido, this is a sign that you need to lengthen the time frame between ejaculations. If, on the other hand, you still have plenty of sexual energy after coming, then the timing of your discharge was appropriate. Although for most men there is no point in refraining from ejaculation indefinitely, learning to leave a sexual exchange feeling energetically invigorated rather than sexually depleted may be the single most important thing a man can do to reclaim his sexual vitality.

Male clients of mine are often curious to know how often I ejaculate. But the more relevant question is: How often do I have sex *without* emitting? I don't mind admitting that I seldom ejaculate, but when I do, it's usually after countless implosive orgasms. At that point, I enjoy the ritual of releasing the discharge in a ceremonial context as a conscious and loving offering to my partner. Though I still value self-pleasuring as a vehicle for generating sexual energy, ejaculating when I masturbate has become unthinkable. Over time and with experience, I have found that the brief rush of pleasure doesn't come close to compensating for the uncomfortable aftermath I experience—especially without any inflowing energy compensation from my female partner.

CHAPTER 6

G-SPOT MASSAGE

Another noteworthy experience from my first tantric workshop was my formal introduction to G-spot massage. Tantric teachings have long specified that all women possess two poles, or hot spots, on their bodies. One is the northern external pole, the clitoris. The other is the lesser-known internal southern pole, the G-spot. Some people feel that these classifications are too limiting, that the human sexual response is so rich, fluid, and varied that it's impossible to declare any absolutes. After all, it may be entirely possible for women to have more than two hot spots—human sexuality is a varied, mystical beast, and there is no good reason to get stuck with any more limiting beliefs.

A BRIEF HISTORY OF THE G-SPOT CONTROVERSY

Believe it or not, there has been considerable controversy about whether or not the G-spot even exists. In the past, many male doctors denied its existence, and the debate over the focal point of female sexual arousal have stirred many scientific arguments. Though Freud's theories aren't too popular with feminists, he was at least on the right track with his assertion that women were capable of both clitoral and vaginal orgasms. According to Freud, one kind results from vaginal penetration, and the other from clitoral stimulation. Unfortunately, Freud's explanation was quite judgmental. He regarded clitoral orgasm as masculine and immature while vaginal orgasms were considered feminine and fully mature. Freud apparently was unfamiliar with full-body, implosive orgasms.

I can understand where Freud was coming from, since the clitoral orgasm closely resembles the normal male ejaculation orgasm. Though it may be intensely pleasurable, it is brief, localized, and fails to lead to rapture or bliss. On the other hand, many women who have experienced the difference between the clitoral orgasm and the deeper, more fulfilling vaginal (G-spot) orgasm will never be satisfied with the lesser of the two.

GRAFENBERG WAS ASTUTE

In spite of Alfred Kinsey's extensive research, he erroneously chose to assume that sexual arousal for women revolved solely around the clitoris, believing it to be the only significant area of female sexual sensitivity. While Dr. Grafenberg agreed with Kinsey that the clitoris is indeed a hotspot for female sexual sensitivity, he recognized that there is an area of extreme sensitivity in the vagina, too. Grafenberg was the first modern physician to describe this trigger point for female orgasm. He noted that it is located on the anterior wall of the ceiling of the vagina, about two inches from the entrance. Many women are aware when a finger or penis loses contact with this area and adjust themselves to this by changing positions. For this astute observation, the Grafenberg spot, or G-spot for short, was named after him.

I'd be remiss if I didn't point out that the tantra community here in Northern California where I live refers to the G-spot as the Goddess spot.

KINSEY, MASTERS AND JOHNSON WERE ALL OFF-TRACK

Believe it or not, in the 1960s, famed researchers Masters and Johnson assured us that the female orgasm involves only the clitoris, making it the sole focus of feminine erotic arousal. To Masters and Johnson, the vaginal orgasm was a myth. Neither Masters and Johnson, nor Kinsey, had any idea that the G-spot existed, even after many years of investigating human sexuality. I still find that to be pretty amazing!

PERRY AND WHIPPLE HONOR GRAFENBERG

It was left to medical researchers Perry and Whipple in 1980 to announce to the world that there is a spot within the vagina that is extremely sensitive to deep pressure. They named the area in honor of Grafenberg. Of course, they were unaware that the spot had been identified in ancient *tantric* texts as the *kunda gland*, where ecstatic energy is said to reside. Perry and Whipple knew that the clitoris was one hotspot that could trigger orgasm, but not the *only* one. They had found the G-spot in every one of more than four hundred women that they examined. They observed that when properly stimulated, the G-spot swells, precipitating orgasm in many women.

At this point in time, the evidence is conclusive. The G-spot not only exists, but it is a major trigger point for female orgasm.

GENITAL ARMORING

Women vary greatly in their responses to G-spot massage. In a typical session, a woman may experience anything from intense emotional and physical pain to rapture and sexual ecstasy. In order to understand why, it's helpful to have a clear understanding of *armoring*: a process whereby past traumatic experiences are stored in the muscular tissues of the body. If you have ever received a deep-tissue massage, you know that during the sometimes painful probing of deep tissues, the simplest touch to some seemingly innocuous part of the body may release a torrent of emotion and long-suppressed memory.

Though most people are unaware of it, the male and female sex organs are just as prone to armoring as the rest of the body. Because the G-spot is so sensitive and well-hidden, it is believed to be a perfect receptacle for storing sexual and emotional trauma. The so-called negative emotions like fear, anger, rage, shame, and guilt often reside in, or are in close proximity to, the anal and genital areas in what has come to be known as *genital armoring*. Armoring causes the tissues to harden, creating tension and blocking energy in the area that's been traumatized. By armoring itself, the body attempts to protect itself from pain, but in the process, the area in question becomes so desensitized that it reduces the person's capacity for pleasure.

In other words, traces of the emotional content of every unsatisfactory sexual experience has been recorded in the muscular tissues of your genitals in a nearly imperceptible way.

Though they are seldom aware of it, if a woman has had painful sexual experiences, her initial response to being touched may be pain, as if she has a bruise or a cut. If she perseveres, however, and she and her partner go slowly, lovingly, and tenderly, the sore spot inside her will heal, and with it her past wounds. Healing herself in this way can awaken a power in her that she has never known.

Sometimes, it can take weeks or months of G-spot healing before ecstatic pleasure is experienced. Now and then, a woman may feel pleasant sensations the first few times her G-spot is massaged, but then it will suddenly become *hypersensitive*. For this reason, the healing partner must be in close emotional contact in order to be highly responsive to her feelings. The healer must lighten his or her touch, or even withdraw if necessary, until she can tolerate more sensation. If she persists, over time, her tolerance will expand and her potential for pleasure will surely increase.

In her book *The Art of Sexual Ecstasy*, Margo Anand speculates that G-spot armoring may result from pushing for an orgasm and not achieving it. Whenever a woman becomes stimulated and aroused, yet *fails* to achieve a full orgasm, she experiences sexual frustration.

I am reminded here of an Osho quote that seems appropriate to this discussion:

"Ninety percent of womankind are angry, nagging and bitchy because their deepest orgasmic needs are never met."

Anand goes on to say:

"Armoring may also occur as a result of faking orgasms, painful medical interventions like caesarian births or hysterectomies, from performance anxiety, by giving in to feelings of sexual inadequacy, from feelings of guilt about masturbation, from forceful male fingering, from sexual intercourse without sufficient foreplay, from abortions, or from making love when not in the mood."

And what about all the women who have been molested, raped, or otherwise sexually abused? No wonder so many women fail to enjoy sexual intercourse. For many women, it can be either a frighteningly painful experience, or one characterized by numbness and insensitivity that renders their vagina only minimally responsive to stimulation from the penis.

G-SPOT MASSAGE: A NEW KIND OF INTIMATE CONNECTION

So what can be done to dissolve genital armoring? How can a woman free herself from the imprints left by negative sexual experiences? How can she transform pain into pleasure? The answer is a series of G-spot massages that provide loving touches from a conscientious person. Only then will a woman be able to experience optimum sexual pleasure.

G-spot massage is an intimate connection of a new kind in our culture. However, because of the dynamic nature of the emotional releases a woman may experience as the armoring yields, it can be quite scary and unpredictable. Remember that psychic wounds often reside inside the vagina. A woman may respond emotionally, even violently in some instances, when the tense muscular tissue begins to soften and relax. For this reason, a dramatic emotional shock may await the unwary initiate if they are unprepared. There can be no doubt that G-spot massage is potentially an explosive and transformational experience.

GENITAL HEALING IS EMPOWERING

Genital healing has the potential to empower a woman in extraordinary ways. Not only can it transform pain into pleasure; it can illuminate her life and provide the opportunity for major psychological breakthroughs. For her, it is a marvelous opportunity to experience increased awareness on many levels. For a woman to receive the optimum level of healing, she will be called upon to tune into her sensory perceptions, or what is called her "feeling mind," as much as possible. She must get out of the thinking mode, out of her head, as this is not a cerebral experience but an effort to expand her sensory and emotional capacities. Identifying with thoughts is a distraction in a process like this, since it tends to isolate a woman from her feelings. As old memories and repressed feelings emerge, she is encouraged to let go of the past and stay open to what is happening now.

LOCATING THE G-SPOT

Though you may have heard of the G-spot, you may have never attempted to locate it, let alone heal it. Likewise, some women are equally ignorant of its location and its potential for healing. It is quite difficult for a woman to access her own G-spot without the help of a partner. As far as *massaging* it and awakening its healing potential, it's probably just too physically awkward to accomplish alone unless a woman makes use of one of the massage tools designed for this purpose. Manufacturers are now creating vibrators and dildos that are curved to match the natural shape of the vagina with attachments for contacting the G-spot. But for women who shun sex toys, or prefer flesh-and-blood fingers, the support of a playmate is essential.

If a woman is lying on her back, it's hard for her to contact her G-spot, since gravity tends to pull the internal organs down and away from the vaginal entrance. Unless she has long fingers and a short vaginal canal, the possibility of comfortably reaching it is remote. But by squatting and exploring the upper front wall of the vagina while pressing up towards the navel with a couple of fingers from the inside, and pressing down just above the pubic bone with the other hand, she can massage the spot.

To the fingers, the G-spot feels like a small bean located directly behind the pubic bone, front and center on the ceiling of the vagina. It's generally located about two inches into the vagina, although the exact size and location varies. If you could imagine a small clock inside the vagina with twelve o'clock pointing towards the navel, most women would find the G-spot located in an area between eleven and one o'clock.

THE G-SPOT IS QUITE WELL HIDDEN

While the clitoris tends to protrude from the surrounding tissue, the G-spot lies embedded deep inside the vaginal wall, quite well hidden. Only when it is stimulated does it become engorged and swollen. At that point, it feels firmer to the touch than the surrounding tissue, almost ridged with well-defined edges in contrast to the smoother skin lining the rest of the vagina. As a matter of fact, it feels much like the areola of an excited nipple. When aroused, it swells anywhere from the size of a dime to the size of a half dollar. Size, however, has no bearing on the level of responsiveness. There is no need to worry: small G-spots, like small penises, can still generate plenty of pleasure.

EMPTY THE BLADDER FIRST

When the G-spot is initially contacted, women often feel a burning sensation, or a sudden need to urinate, since the spot lies so close to the bladder. These feelings usually pass in thirty seconds or so, after which more pleasurable feelings may arise. Because of this phenomenon, it is helpful for women to empty their bladder prior to the massage to ease any fear of urinating. I also recommend placing several soft, fluffy towels under the woman's buttocks to let her know that you are prepared for the release of fluids, since this type of massage is known to trigger *female* ejaculation. Let her know that bodily fluids are a natural part of sexual excitement—and that the appearance of fluids just adds to the fun. Hopefully this reduces any embarrassment that she might have about wetting the bed. For practical reasons, though, emptying the bladder helps to isolate and identify the G-spot sensations as distinct from those of a full bladder.

THE ELUSIVE G-SPOT

One of the challenges in G-spot massage, particularly with someone who is not a lover, is creating an experience that does not seem overly clinical, like a gynecological exam. For best results, the G-spot should be massaged only when a woman is very aroused. Therefore, the best times to contact the spot is just before, during, or just after orgasm, depending on the woman's preference. If the G-spot is massaged prematurely, the sensations may not be particularly pleasant. The tricky part is how to get a woman prepared for her G-spot experience. Experience tells me that it is helpful to get her energy moving first. One great way to prepare her is to offer a relaxing, sensuous massage that will serve to awaken her whole body. Activities such as dancing or gentle yoga stretching are great preparation for many women.

Some women may prefer a warm bath, meditation, or perhaps eye-gazing with a partner as a means of deepening the connection. It's really important to keep communicating with each other as the process unfolds. Once orgasm begins, the G-spot is capable of receiving considerable pressure that may help the orgasm deepen and expand. However, whether or not an orgasm is forthcoming, as long as her vagina is sufficiently lubricated and she is open to receiving, finesse (and a gentle hand) is a wise approach. Once the healer finds the spot, he or she should apply light-to-medium pressure and hold the contact point with the fingers motionless in their position inside the vagina. The other hand may either exert light pressure on the clitoris, or rest between her breasts, a contact that emphasizes the *heart-genital connection*. Another pleasing option is to press down just above the pubic bone that accesses the G-spot from outside and above. This will give her a better chance to integrate the sensations and process her feelings before deeper stimulation begins.

Until a woman is fully aroused, the G-spot will remain small and soft and virtually indistinguishable from the surrounding tissue. This may explain why this sensitive hotspot has been overlooked for so long by the medical profession. During the course of a normal gynecological exam, the area of the G-spot is usually palpated, but never intentionally stimulated as a matter of medical ethics. Remember, physicians are taught to avoid procedures that might cause their patients to become sexually aroused. For this reason alone, it's easy to understand why the G-spot has been mostly overlooked. After all, it's not visible, and just as the penis does not usually swell during a medical exam, neither does the G-spot. If you think about it, if a doctor didn't know any better, he or she would be forced to conclude that a man's penis is always soft, droopy, and only two or three inches long simply based on their own observations.

THE IMPORTANCE OF EXPLORING DIFFERENT POSITIONS

Over the years, I've become convinced that contacting the G-spot during intercourse is essential for optimizing a woman's pleasure. Women who do not experience orgasm during intercourse could benefit by exploring different sexual positions until they find one that allows direct stimulation of this zone. Consider that men exhibit wide variations in terms of the angle of their erections and the size and shape of their penis. Women must find what works best for them. It should be noted that a man who has an erect penis that lies flat against his belly might very well contact a woman's G-spot perfectly in missionary position, whereas this might not be the case in other more acrobatic scenarios. On the other hand, for some women, contact with their G-spot is more likely from the rear-entry position (sometimes known as "doggy-style"), and in others from the woman on top position ("cowgirl," or "reverse cowgirl"). Not only does the physiology of the partners and the positioning for intercourse play a role in the stimulation of the G-spot, but the *cooperation* of the partners plays a part as well. It may just be that the frame of the perfect lover is based on the compatibility of the physiological characteristics, along with the couple's willingness to improvise, experiment, and communicate.

G-SPOT MASSAGE: A PERFECT STRATEGY FOR PROLONGED SEX PLAY

Of course, even perfectly compatible sex organs won't work as long as the G-spot remains armored or insensitive. I would encourage any couple in a sexual relationship to explore G-spot massage for a couple of reasons. First and foremost, most women *need* this kind of healing work. Virtually all women (and many men) have some degree of armoring. Second, even if they *don't* have any armoring, this form of deep-tissue massage offers women the possibility of extraordinary orgasmic pleasure.

G-spot massage also serves as a wonderful way for a man to prolong sexual play and lavish unbridled attention on his female partner. Here's one scenario that works for me: during sexual intercourse, as soon as I approach peak arousal, I withdraw my penis from her vagina (coitus interruptus), preventing the possibility of an unwanted ejaculation. Remember, arousal does not require a release. I position myself between my partner's legs and continue to stimulate her manually. I alternate with clitoral and G-spot massage, intermittently asking for feedback and receiving direction from her. Though I am still aroused from intercourse, this is my chance to relax into my arousal and let go of any fatigue or tension that I may have unconsciously created in my own body.

I proceed to pleasure her with conscious, loving touches. When I lose about 30 percent of my erection, I ask permission to re-enter her. With her permission, this cycle may be repeated again and again. I alternate between G-spot massage and intercourse, the sexual energy gradually heightening toward fever pitch. Of course, my first priority is always to shower my partner with love and affection and to see to it that she is fully satisfied. This strategy works for both of us. She gets to receive as many thrills as she wishes and I get to feel successful and fulfilled knowing I have pleased her.

THE HEALER'S ATTITUDE

Over the years, I've come to realize the importance of creating a safe space to optimize an individual's healing potential. When people come to me for sexual healing, they are trustingly placing themselves in my hands. Since sexual healing is such an extraordinarily intimate experience and the person receiving it is in such an extremely vulnerable position, it is imperative to make that person feel as safe as humanly possible. Ideally, the people receiving the healing not only feel comfortable around me, but also enjoy spending time with me. If they really trust me, it's much easier for them to let go of fears and surrender into the process.

Experience tells me that the unwillingness or inability to let go of the past is the basis for many sexual dysfunctions. Fully letting go, however, can be scary, since it represents loss of control. As a healer, a relaxed and loving attitude works best. Love and acceptance are the greatest healers. You can be certain that no healing ever truly takes place without it. An important point to understand is that you do not need to try to *create* love, since love is your true essence. A healing session then becomes an exercise in not impeding the natural energetic flow of divine love. Really, only one thing is necessary: do not block the energy!

HEALERS DO NOT HEAL

The healer's role is one of absolute service. The healing of the G-spot requires the conscious, loving touch of a person who wishes to be in service to the living goddess. It really doesn't matter whether the massage is performed by a man or a woman, but patience and sensitivity is a must. A proper intention for a healer is to be a clear channel for the rejuvenating life force energy to come through. Be very clear that as a healer, you do not heal anyone. People heal themselves when they are ready. As a healer, you are not the source of the healing power, but rather a *channel* for it. As people relax and let go, it is the life force energy directed by its own intelligence that provides healing. Healers merely facilitate the healing process by acting as a catalyst for those people most interested in healing themselves. A healer attempts to create the optimum conditions in which healing can occur, but that's all!

Here's what Osho, formerly Rajneesh (and perhaps the greatest tantric master of the twentieth century), had to say about healing in his opus, simply titled *The Book*:

"*Healing is a delicate dimension. And the delicacy consists in the healer not doing anything in it. The healer is not really a healer because he is not a doer. Healing happens through him. He has just to annihilate himself. To be a healer really means not to be. The less you are, the better healing will happen. The more you are, the more the passage is blocked. God, or the totality, or whatever name you prefer, is the healer. The whole is the healer."*

DO NOT BE ATTACHED TO THE OUTCOME

With the proper attitude, miracles can happen. But do not place too much emphasis on the outcome of a session. Have a strong desire to help, but don't let the ego become involved. In this way, you maximize your ability to be a clear channel. If you focus too hard on achieving a certain result instead of giving yourself over to the experience, you are like a glass of muddy water, stirred by the ego and caught up in self-importance. When you are able to be still inside, everything settles to the bottom and the water becomes transparent and clear.

CHAPTER 7

FEMALE EJACULATION

I find it fascinating that men place so much emphasis on their own ejaculations, often to their detriment, while virtually ignoring women's ejaculatory capacity. The world would be a much different (and dare I say, better) place if men ejaculated less and women ejaculated more!

While the discovery of the G-spot may rank first in importance of all the "new" sexual discoveries, female ejaculation is more observably dramatic. While female ejaculation is new to modern sexology, tantric texts mentioned its existence thousands of years ago. Female ejaculate, or *amrita* as it was called, was viewed as fine nectar prized by the erotic connoisseur for its invigorating qualities.

Disregarding the many descriptions of female ejaculation in both medical and popular literature throughout history, some contemporary sexologists still dismiss the phenomenon, often diagnosing it as "urinary stress incontinence." If they had taken the trouble to examine the ejaculate, they would have noticed that it doesn't look or smell like urine at all. Furthermore, it is difficult to explain why women who ejaculate tend to have unusually strong *pubococcygeus*, or PC muscles, while urinary stress incontinence is associated with *weak* PC muscles. It's hard to believe that these contradictions could go unnoticed by doctors who are presumably trained in the scientific method. But when it comes to sex, apparently even the most logical minds can miss what's right in front of their nose.

It wasn't until the 1978 publication of an article in the *Journal of Sex Research* that opinions began to change. The research of scientists Sevely and Bennett suggested that women *can* ejaculate, and that one component of the fluid expelled by women through the urethra is prostatic fluid. They did no chemical analysis, but they speculated that female ejaculation, like male ejaculation, contributes to erotic pleasure. What is known is that female ejaculation is most often, though not always, triggered at the peak of orgasm. Therefore, it seems to have no lubricating significance, otherwise it would be produced earlier in the arousal process. Scientific research has not yet identified any specific purpose this fluid might serve other than sexual pleasure.

Considering the relatively new notion that women might enjoy sexual pleasure for its own sake, there has been little incentive for male scientists to concern themselves with either female orgasm or female ejaculate. While male ejaculate is called semen, female ejaculate has no name, and so it has quickly vanished from science texts. No wonder its existence was denied for so long. The same myopic bunch of doubting Thomases who denied the existence of the G-spot also denounced the *possibility* of female ejaculation.

For example, in 1966, Masters and Johnson wrote that female ejaculation is "an erroneous but widespread concept." Earlier, Kinsey stated that:

"Since the prostate gland and the seminal vesicles are only vestigial structures in the female, she does not actually ejaculate. Muscular contractions in the vagina following orgasm may squeeze out some genital secretions, and in some cases eject them with some force. This is frequently referred to, in erotic literature, as an ejaculation in the female, but the term cannot strictly be used in that connection."

Germaine Greer, a prominent voice in the women's liberation movement of the 1970s, asserted that:

"All kinds of false ideas are still in circulation about women, although they were disproved years ago. Many men refuse to relinquish the notion of female ejaculation, which although it has a prestigious history, is utterly fanciful."

The likely reason so many authorities doubt the existence of female ejaculation is that while it's a highly visible (and visceral) phenomenon, most have never personally observed it. For one thing, most women do not ejaculate regularly. Ladas, Whipple, and Perry report that when they first began asking women if they ever ejaculated, only about 10 percent said they did. Over time, with increased public awareness, this figure has risen to about 40 percent.

Relaxation and emotional security are crucial for women to become aroused and stimulated enough to ejaculate. As I've already stated, female ejaculation requires strong sex muscles capable of "bearing down" or pushing out with great force. Also, while some women can ejaculate rather quickly, most require strong G-spot stimulation for thirty minutes, or even an hour or more, before they experience release. This requires a lover who has either great sexual stamina or the dexterity to perform G-spot massage. Though some women report they can ejaculate from clitoral stimulation alone, the vast majority requires lengthy G-spot stimulation. However, if these requirements are met, any healthy, sexually open woman can ejaculate.

I predict that as more women become conscious of their expanded sexual potential, the incidence of female ejaculation will increase. There are now many "closet ejaculators" coming out to share their stories with friends. In fact, here in the San Francisco Bay area where I live, there are several groups of women who get together on a regular basis to share G-spot massage with each other. There are also several sexually explicit videos made by women to teach the "sisterhood" how to ejaculate, including one where I demonstrate my own G-spot massage technique.

Female ejaculation involves the ejection of fluid gushing, squirting, seeping, spurting, or flowing through the urethra, usually at the moment of orgasm. One of the amazing characteristics of female ejaculate is the copious amount of fluid that some women release. As an example, my lover, who admittedly has a strong sexual capacity, produces as much as a cupful at a time. Many times she has literally soaked the sheets, and we've regretted our failure to place towels down before our lovemaking began, especially after having just washed the bedding!

During a typical sexual exchange, she may ejaculate three, four, or even more times, mostly during intercourse, but also from G-spot massage. As a show of love and appreciation for her, I always volunteer to sleep on the wet spot.

A HOT MINERAL BATH

During intercourse, the release of my lover's nectar drenches my penis and testicles in what I like to think of as a wonderful, hot, mineral bath. During manual stimulation, I have a bird's eye view of my lover pushing out like she would if she was giving birth, thus triggering the release of amrita. She says that often the contractions are an involuntary response to arousal, but that sometimes she intentionally initiates the bearing down when she feels the release is imminent. Let's be clear that women cannot ejaculate on command: they can attempt it, but ejaculation will happen in its own time, since it is directed not by the mind, but by the intelligence of the body. Nevertheless, a great method of facilitating ejaculation is to massage the G-spot lovingly while encouraging an attitude of surrender and relaxation. Sometimes, it may take a series of massage sessions before a woman can begin ejaculating on a regular basis.

It's important to make the point that many women who do not yet ejaculate can experience completely fulfilling orgasms. Just as a woman can orgasm without ejaculating, she can also ejaculate without having an orgasm. While there are many women who experience orgasm and ejaculation together, many do not. There must not be any pressure on a woman to perform in any particular way. The best perspective for a man to have is that it's great if you do, and it's great if you don't. Of course, the same can be said about orgasm. Women, like men, respond best to heartfelt expressions of love rather than expectations and performance demands.

SOLVING THE MYSTERY

Personally, I don't really concern myself with *where* ejaculate comes from, or what it consists of. If it contributes to sexual pleasure, I say, "Let the juices flow." But if your curiosity or your hygienic concerns demand more information, you're in luck. Recent research has discovered both the biological origin and the chemical makeup of female ejaculate. In most studies, researchers found significant differences between the ejaculate and the urine of the subjects. In some instances, the female ejaculate was found to be extraordinarily similar to male prostatic fluid and is thought to originate from the female equivalent of the prostate gland, known as the urethral glands; that is, from the glands and ducts surrounding the female urethra.

Dr. Gary Shubach was determined to establish the origin of the fluids that women ejaculate. His subjects were seven women who regularly ejaculated. He catheterized these women in order to collect any fluid coming from the bladder while they stimulated themselves to orgasm and ejaculation. He found that more than 95 percent of the fluid that women expelled during sexual arousal originates in the bladder and passes through the urethra. However, the ejaculatory fluid proved to be very different from the urine samples collected *prior* to arousal. It had a greatly reduced concentration of urea. Dr. Shubach concluded that female ejaculate is "an altered form of urine," and that the body changes the chemical composition of this fluid during sexual excitement. Some women were also observed to secrete a thicker, milky, semen-like fluid from the urethral glands, so it appears that the ejaculatory fluid originates not from either the bladder or the urethral glands, but from *both*.

What is certain is that female ejaculate does not have the color, taste, or smell of urine. It has been variously described as colorless, clear, or milky—but no woman, no matter how much she was afraid that she was urinating, ever described the fluid as yellow in color. Yet, many women who ejaculate report that they were embarrassed to think they might have urinated, and so they learned, sadly, to suppress their own enjoyment of nature's sexy gift.

Some women report that they ejaculate every time they make love, others only occasionally. Some women ejaculate with certain partners, but not with others, and in certain positions, but not in others. Some women have detected a cyclical pattern possibly related to the phases of their menstrual cycle.

APPRECIATION, SHAME, AND DISBELIEF

Attitudes about bodily fluids—specifically female ejaculate—vary from disgust and revulsion to appreciation and unconditional acceptance. I've always seen my lover's sexual secretions as a natural turn-on. To me, the release of her fluids represents a woman's way of surrendering control. That's what I find so exciting! So it was a shock for me to read in "The G-Spot and Other Recent Discoveries about Human Sexuality" that some women have been humiliated by partners critical of their release of sexual fluids. No wonder some women learn to suppress orgasms. For example, one woman's boyfriend was so disgusted by her "urinating" during orgasm that he left her. Thinking that there was something wrong with her, she consulted a male physician. He compounded her problem by suggesting that she had "a physiological problem experienced by many women who lose control of their bladder during orgasm." Because of this, she avoided sexual contact for years and spent a great deal of time and money on unnecessary psychological counseling.

ONE OF THE SADDEST STORIES IN THE BOOK:

"I couldn't have relations with my husband without wetting my bed. My husband was no help. He kept telling me to go to the bathroom before coming to bed. After a divorce and a change of partners, I was mortified when my new man accused me of urinating on him."

Happily, there were also reports from women whose relationships were enhanced by their ejaculations. One woman who had been married for thirty-eight years wrote:

"Over the years, I have ejaculated often. I have been a virtual geyser of fluids, enough to wet the bed, different from lubrication, with a distinctive odor. It usually occurs while I'm on top. Rather than disturbing us, my husband and I have always related to this phenomenon as heightened pleasure, often accompanied by multiple orgasms for both of us. I always assumed naively that other women were having similar experiences."

Now that the word is out about women's ability to ejaculate, I hope to see a change in attitude with more people enjoying this gift with gratitude and appreciation. Whenever I have the opportunity, I drink deeply of this mystical feminine nectar. My own experience tells me that even a little taste serves as a powerful elixir that I find extremely erotic and rejuvenating.

CHAPTER 8

HOW TO AVOID MALE EJACULATION

When I first decided to adopt non-ejaculatory sex as my new sexual paradigm, I knew it would require a profound mental shift if I were to achieve any measure of success. Charles reminded me that I create my future with the power of intention—by consciously determining the path my future would take. That being the case, successfully mastering non-ejaculatory sex would have to begin with the right mental approach, namely: *"I will not ejaculate."* You may have seen bumper stickers that say, *"Shift Happens."* I'm proof that it does.

I began my non-ejaculatory sex life intending to switch my emphasis from a lifetime of *explosive* ejaculations to the higher sex play of *implosive* orgasms. I knew that initially it would be a bit tricky to overcome the habit of coming, so I felt that it was important to not put too much pressure on myself to succeed. I would make mistakes along the way—just like Charles warned me I would. But I knew I would have the rest of my life to practice. This became my mantra.

MALE EJACULATION IS A TWO-PART PROCESS

Male ejaculation is a two-part process. In the *emission phase*, the prostate gland, already swollen with sexual fluids from the energy of arousal, contracts and empties semen into the urethra. As men, we experience the emission phase as the point of no return. So whatever ejaculation control method you choose to employ (and there are several), it must be activated *just before* the emission phase begins. This is the point just before the prostate gland begins its familiar pumping action.

The second part of the male ejaculation process is the *expulsion phase*. In the expulsion phase, a rhythmic, wavelike muscular contraction of the pelvic muscles propels semen through the urethra and out the penis.

Every man is familiar with these delightful involuntary contractions: this is genital orgasm.

BEGINNING, INTERMEDIATE, AND ADVANCED METHODS

As I've said before, there are several ways to avoid an unwanted male genital release. In this chapter, I will describe three of them. They all work (when properly employed), but some are more user-friendly and efficient than others.

A BEGINNING METHOD

If you habitually come too soon, this may be a good place for you to start. The *withdrawal method* is quite easy to perform, but it is the least desirable because it involves "coitus interruptus," the fancy Latin term for pulling out of the vagina before you ejaculate. As soon as a man feels that he is getting too excited for his own good, he simply withdraws his penis from the vagina for at least sixty seconds or until he feels that the danger of coming has passed. Ideally, he should wait until he has lost about 30 percent of his erection. At that point, it is deemed safe to re-enter her sacred space and resume slow, gentle movements, only enough to stay hard. When the point of no return is again approached, another withdrawal is needed. A man can do this as often as he needs to. As he gains experience, he will find he needs to withdraw less often, eventually needing to perform this preventative measure only on rare occasions.

Masters and Johnson encouraged some men to use the withdrawal method. The hope was that intercourse could be extended, so that women who needed a longer arousal time in order to achieve orgasm would have a better chance of being sexually satisfied. The key for men is being able to discern when climax is approaching and withdrawing before that point. This is vital, not just to avoid coming too soon, but especially when both partners choose to rely on withdrawal as a means of birth control.

AN INTERMEDIATE METHOD

This method involves locating the prostate point and applying direct pressure at the appropriate time. The prostate point can be found precisely midway between the anus and the scrotum. There you will find an indentation approximately the size of a pea. Using the index and middle finger of the left hand, men can prevent semen loss by reaching around behind the buttocks with one hand—prior to climax—and pressing hard against the prostate point for four seconds or more while taking a big inhale through the nose. The applied pressure prevents semen from entering the urethra, sending it instead to be rerouted and ultimately reabsorbed into the bloodstream, and circulated to the rest of the body.

Don't be afraid to apply deep pressure here. I've also successfully used my right hand, so experiment and see what works best. Once again—timing is vital. You must use this direct pressure method *before* the emission phase begins. Like the withdrawal method, it's better to apply this method too soon rather than too late. I recommend that you explore this area of your body until you become very familiar with this point. Self-pleasuring is a great way to practice.

Once you become proficient with this method, you will develop the ability to experience what is known as a "dry ejaculation," or what Steven Chang, author of *The Tao of Sexology* calls an "injaculation." When you injaculate, it feels exactly like you're coming. You can feel the prostate gland performing its delightful pumping action, but since the urethra is being pinched off by direct pressure, semen cannot enter the urethra. Instead, the semen is redirected inside the body. If you are successful, there will be no semen loss. It certainly beats the withdrawal method, since you can stay inside your lover's vagina throughout the entire sexual exchange, but the downside is that it can be enormously clumsy to perform in the heat of the sexual dance. However, the good news is that once you've sufficiently developed your sex muscles, you can leave this method, as well as the withdrawal method, behind forever.

Before I describe how men can use their sex muscles to avoid coming, pay attention to a warning from Margo Anand. In her book, *The Art of Sexual Ecstasy*, Margo offers this reminder to men:

"Before lovemaking, many men decide they will stop before the point of no return to avoid coming. But in the heat of sex, their female partner gets

so excited that the man receives no support from her to resist the final rush. Or, in a moment of rising sexual passion, he becomes so desirous for release himself that he overrides his previous intention not to come. He thinks, 'Ah, I'll do it next time; this feels too good.'"

The key point is that you have to want to avoid coming and you must stay committed to the process. According to Mantak Chia in his book, *Taoist Secrets of Love: Cultivating Male Sexual Energy*, the average man comes five thousand times in his lifetime. *Enough already!* Try something different. If you keep doing the same things, you'll keep getting the same results.

AN ADVANCED METHOD

This third and more efficient method involves a sustained contraction of the internal muscles used in sex. Once you have mastered this technique, there will be no need to ever withdraw from the vagina to prevent coming. There will be no need for any more daunting attempts at locating the prostate point with your fingers while immersed in the heat of arousal with a passionate woman.

STRENGTHENING THE SEX MUSCLES

First, some background: many of you engage in various activities in the pursuit of physical fitness. You might go to health clubs to tone and strengthen your muscles, so you can look and feel better. While this type of exercise is focused on strengthening the external muscles, for many practitioners of the sexual arts, the focus shifts to toning the *internal* muscles—specifically those used in sex.

Weak sex muscles not only compromise a man's ability to provide complete female sexual satisfaction, but they also inhibit sexual ecstasy. To put it succinctly: weak sex muscles reduce the capacity for sexual pleasure and genital health for both men and women.

The sex muscles consist of two anal sphincter muscles and the pubococcygeus (PC), a group of pelvic muscles that move as a unit, contracting involuntarily about once per second during genital climax. The sex muscles create the pelvic floor, which connects the anus and the genitals.

KEGEL EXERCISES

In the late 1940s, pioneering gynecologist Arnold Kegel discovered the value of strong PC muscles for sexual health and pleasure. Tantric and Taoist practitioners, however, had been well aware of this muscle group and its role in proper sexual function thousands of years ago. In fact, many of yoga's most important exercises were designed to train and strengthen this specific muscle group.

Kegel made his discovery quite by accident while treating women who had trouble controlling their bladders. He hoped to help them avoid surgery by strengthening their PC muscles through a basic exercise program that has come to bear his name. Not only were the exercises helpful in warding off surgery, but many women reported a very interesting side effect. The exercises left them significantly sexually aroused—and some of them began to experience orgasm for the first time in their lives.

In conscious sexual practice, well-developed sex muscles are looked upon as "guardians" of the life force energy. These muscles prevent energy from "leaking" outside the body. The Taoist sages thought of the human torso as a bucket of energy with two "holes" at the bottom: the anus and the urethra. When the sex muscles are weak, flaccid, and poorly developed, energy may seep out of those holes—a bit like having slow leaks in the front and rear tires of your car.

It's a fact that a flabby, undeveloped muscle is not very responsive to physical stimulation. Typically, men with weak sex muscles experience puny localized ejaculations accompanied by fatigue. Women in a similar situation are often unable to achieve orgasm at all. Happily, like any other muscles in the body, the sex muscles respond quickly to proper exercise and training.

Highly motivated students of the sexual arts exercise these muscles on a regular basis. Like athletes, they hone their skills with repeated practice of very specialized movements. A daily training program for a few months can transform a person's sexual health and serve as a great source of empowerment. As my own sex muscles grew stronger, I experienced a huge increase in sexual pleasure—and so will you.

BE A COUCH POTATO IF YOU WISH

If you don't like strenuous exercise and have a hard time getting motivated, rest assured that sexercises are easy to perform. You don't have to be an athlete. You can be a couch potato and literally work out, or in this case work *in*, while you lie down on the couch. They don't take up much time, either—just five minutes a day will suffice.

The physical benefits of strong sex muscles are numerous. In addition to creating firmer erections, they enhance lovemaking to the point whereby the male ejaculation process becomes a conscious choice to come, or not, rather than an involuntary reflex. Strong sex muscles shorten the refractory phase (that unfortunate interval after ejaculation when men have difficulty maintaining an erection). But more importantly, by preventing unwanted ejaculation, they provide men with the ability to experience multiple full-body orgasms *without ejaculating*.

By now you know that avoiding male ejaculation is the key to extended pleasure. In addition, strong sex muscles rejuvenate the reproductive organs of men and women by improving blood flow to the genitals and revitalizing the tissues of the uro-genital tract. Strong sex muscles increase orgasmic capacity. They intensify sexual feelings and prolong arousal, thus stimulating the release of beneficial sex hormones that are associated with youth, health, and longevity.

Women who strengthen their sex muscles increase their vaginal "holding power" by tightening and firming the vaginal muscles. This is particularly important after childbirth, when the vaginal muscles are stretched and in need of toning. Clenching skills not only enable women to achieve genital orgasm more easily, but provide infinitely more pleasure for their male lovers because of the vagina's enhanced gripping action. To put it rather crassly: *Men love tight pussies!*

Toned sex muscles also enhance the lubricating potential of the vagina. With each voluntary contraction of the sex muscles, oxygen-rich blood permeates the vaginal tissue, increasing the potential for lubrication. This is especially important for post-menopausal women who tend to experience vaginal dryness. I've reached the age where some of my close female friends have to deal with this issue. Since vaginal dryness is a common problem in their sex lives, I encourage them to strengthen their sex muscles.

I ask them:

"Why increase the risk of breast or uterine cancer by using synthetic hormonal creams to keep the vagina moist, when simple internal workouts accomplish the same goal without the risks and possible negative side effects?"

Perry and Whipple reported that the stronger a woman's sex muscles, the more likely she will experience orgasm as a result of vaginal stimulation. Women with weak sex muscles either could not achieve orgasm at all, or could achieve orgasm only with direct clitoral stimulation, but not via intercourse. In the same way that athletes with their greater muscular development are generally considered sexy and attractive, strong sex muscles are sexier and more responsive, too.

The PC muscle is the monarch of the sex muscles. It is the base muscle group of the pelvic floor, connecting the anus and genitals. More precisely, it attaches to the pubic bone in the front and stretches to the coccyx, or tailbone, at the base of the spine in the rear. The easiest way to find the muscle is to stop and start the flow as you urinate. This may feel like a valve closing and opening around the genital area. If you pay strict attention, you may also notice a tightening around the anus. Remember, the PC muscle and the anal sphincter muscles move as a unit. You also use the PC muscle to force out the last drop of urine when standing over the toilet. As men squeeze and then relax the PC muscle, the penis bobs up and down. This is particularly noticeable with a firm erection.

Visually, the movement of the PC muscle for women is not quite as dramatic as it is for men. However, a strong PC muscle gives the vagina the viselike ability to firmly grasp a finger, dildo, or penis when the muscle group is squeezed—or even to forcefully push them out of the vagina in some cases. A woman with strong sex muscles can exhibit the "snapping pussy" of popular sexual literature. At least on a purely physical level, she possesses the skills to be the greatest lover of them all because of her ability to milk, grip, fondle, and caress her lover's penis while it is inside her sacred space.

Let's move now to the rear tires, so to speak. The anal sphincters are two rings of muscle less than an inch apart. The outer ring is located at the entrance to the rectum. The inner ring is about three-quarters of an inch inside the rectal canal. These are the muscles that can hold back a bowel movement (or untimely gas) when needed. If I asked you to tighten your anus, you could probably feel the outer ring contracting like a valve closing on itself. However, to feel the inner ring requires more strength. If at first you cannot feel the inner ring at all, don't despair. Until you have practiced, it will take some time before you can feel it contracting.

APPLYING AN ANAL LOCK

The good news for men is that once these inner and outer rings are sufficiently strengthened, applying a timely, sustained, simultaneous contraction of both rings will prevent an unwanted ejaculation. The anal sphincters seal off the urethral duct in the same manner as the direct-pressure method, but without needing to use your hands. A strong contraction will prevent semen from exiting the body. Of course, the sustained clenching action of the anal sphincters, known in yoga as an "anal lock," must stay contracted until the urge to come has passed. As you might imagine, successfully applying the anal lock is a much more user-friendly method of ejaculation control than either the withdrawal or the direct-pressure methods.

INCREASING YOUR ANAL AWARENESS

The anal lock can be applied sitting, standing, or lying down. First, focus your attention precisely at the anus. Remember a time when you had to hold back a bowel movement or hold in an enema. Gradually squeeze the same muscles. Men may experience a pull on their testicles. Women may experience tiny micro-movements around the vaginal lips. Clench and hold for a count of five, then release. Notice if any other muscles are contracting. If they are, then your challenge will be to learn to isolate the anal sphincter muscles so that the only tension is at the anal-pelvic floor. The rest of the body stays relaxed. Keep the belly soft. Overcome the tendency to tighten the buttocks, thighs, jaw, toes, forehead or any other part of the body. You are learning to isolate the anal sphincter muscles that comprise the pelvic floor, and this takes an increase in body awareness and some practice.

CLOSE YOUR EYES AND TUNE IN

Now, gradually squeeze again, a little harder this time. When it feels like the anus is being sucked up and into the body, the anal opening is tightly sealed and you have successfully contracted the inner ring. Hold for a count of five, squeezing tightly before you release the contraction. Tune in to your bodily sensations—and remember that energy follows awareness. In this case, the energy will spread like a warm wave over the anal-pelvic area. Upon releasing the lock, you may experience a subtle feeling of tranquility as the energy moves up the spine to the upper torso. Make this an *inner* experience. It is an exercise in subtle energy awareness. Close your eyes and tune in.

PRACTICE AT RED LIGHTS

As with the anal lock, PC muscle clenching can be practiced anywhere, at any time, without anyone noticing. It can be done sitting, standing, or lying down. I enjoy exercising the PC muscle in such diverse places as a warm bath while pleasuring myself or in my car while stopped at a red light. If you have a partner to make love with, it's exciting to practice during coitus. It will heighten the degree of erotic feelings that both of you experience without the need for pelvic thrusting or any other external movements that might wear you out.

Notice that sexercises needn't take any extra time out of your day. They can be combined with many other activities like watching TV, walking, reading, writing, listening to music, or even while meditating. You can even enjoy public workouts at your health club like I do. While others are pumping iron, and focusing on their external anatomy, I alternate lifting with periods of internal exercise. During the time that is normally used for resting between sets, I perform internal sex muscle contractions. It facilitates the circulation of energy throughout my body, and it definitely improves my workouts. It feels balanced, wholesome, healthy, energizing, erotic, and *fun*.

Like anal locking, PC muscle workouts may involve either sustained clenching or rapid contractions of the PC muscle interspersed with periods of rest. Regardless of which routine you employ, isolating and contracting the sex muscles while the rest of the body stays relaxed is paramount. With practice, you will overcome the tendency to contract an army of muscles along with the sex muscles. Keep practicing, and the ability to isolate the sex muscles will surely emerge.

Here's a six-step training regimen that guarantees success as long as you diligently perform these sexercises daily:

#1. The PC Pulse: Tighten and relax the PC muscle twenty-five times in quick, short bursts, about once per second. Do two sessions per day and gradually build up to a hundred squeezes twice a day. When you can comfortably do one hundred contractions twice a day, add the next step, the PC grip.

#2. The PC Grip: Coordinate your breathing with the movement of the sex muscles. Inhale deeply through the nose as you squeeze your PC muscle tightly to a count of five. Exhale, relax, and let go. Start with ten per session, two sessions per day. Build up to twenty-five each session, twice a day.

#3. Push-Outs: Use your abdominal and PC muscles to bear down or push out as if you were expelling a bowel movement. Inhale and squeeze the PC muscle, then exhale, relax, and let go. Push out again before the next inhale. Continue in this fashion for a couple of minutes. Pushing out, or bearing down, is the key movement that facilitates female ejaculation in women with strong PC muscles.

#4. Red Light/Green Light: Perform the following sexercise at least once a day. Morning is best, since you usually wake up with a full bladder. Start urinating and stop. Start again and stop. Do this until your bladder is empty.

#5. Mirror, Mirror: Stand naked in front of a mirror and contract and relax your PC muscle. Men may observe their penis bobbing up and down, while women may detect tiny movements on the vaginal lips with each squeeze. As the sex muscles strengthen, the movements become more pronounced. Women will find it helpful to practice sexercises with something that will offer resistance: a penis-shaped vibrator, a dildo, or even a finger. Use your imagination. From what I've been told, the most extraordinary experience is to practice when your lover's erect penis is inside you, so let him assist you. My guess is he'll relish the opportunity. It's a tough job, but somebody has to do it.

#6. See-Saw: Men, enter your lover and remain perfectly still. Any position will do, but no friction sex. Stay in passive receptive mode as your lover squeezes and relaxes her PC muscle a minimum of twenty-five times, then reverse the roles. Men, pump your PC muscle twenty-five times or more so that she may receive an exquisite internal massage from your bobbing penis. Remember to keep the rest of your body still during this exercise: no external movements are needed.

Reminder: Anal sphincter contractions can be used instead of PC muscle contractions, or vice-versa. Remember, all the sex muscles move as a unit. The more you practice, the more you sharpen the brain-sex muscle connection until you develop perfect feel and control.

LET YOUR PARTNER BE OF SERVICE TO YOU

If you have a partner, he or she can be a valuable source of feedback in evaluating the strength of your sex muscles. If your partner can feel you contract and relax your sex muscles during intercourse, you'll know they're sufficiently developed. Ask for feedback! Have fun with this!

RELAX THE ANUS AND GENITALS

Men in particular must learn to relax the sex muscles so they can last longer during intercourse. Other than when I am applying the anal lock or consciously squeezing my PC muscle, I'm always reminding myself to relax my anus and genitals. Relaxed sex muscles promote orgasmic flow, while chronically tense sex muscles block the flow, and worse yet, create a sense of urgency for men to ejaculate. As the level of arousal increases and the sexual charge heightens, the feeling of pressure in the genitals heightens accordingly. It's important for men to not only practice strengthening the sex muscles, but also to practice relaxing them. Greater sex muscle awareness will increase a man's staying power.

Though mastering the ability to hold back from a genital release is not as critical for women as for men, women would be wise to keep practicing as well. Holdbacks increase sexual energy and facilitate a joyful, full-body experience. Women always have the option to come if they want to, but I recommend exploring the practice of holding back, since the full-body experience tends to be more memorable than a genital release. Ladies, keep playing with the energy! See what works for you. Remember, you have the rest of your life to practice.

CHAPTER 9

SEXUAL LOVE: THE HEART-GENITAL CONNECTION

One of the most common complaints that I hear from women about their male lovers is that they are just too genital-focused. It's no secret that women crave sexual intimacy; they seek a soulful experience that relates to the heart as well as the groin. Their craving for it is so deep that its absence ensures dissatisfaction at a primal level. Most women would agree there are certainly other considerations that a superior male lover needs to possess beyond mere technique and skill. In other words, no matter how many stimulating tricks a man employs in sex—no matter how accomplished a lover he may be—unless heartfelt love is present, a woman will never feel satisfied to the core—and despite what some men claim, neither will her male partner.

On some level, everybody knows that sex without love leaves you wanting. It's one-dimensional, too limited in emotional scope to create a totally fulfilling experience. How could it be otherwise if the experience is restricted to the genitals? No matter how intense or outrageous the orgasmic discharge, something's missing. Sooner or later, dissatisfaction will creep in. The physical part of the sexual exchange is relatively easy. Sexual love is a bit more complex, however. It requires not just a genital connection, but also the ability to raise sexual energy into the love center. You must involve the heart to create a genuine loving experience.

A MAN'S HEART MAY BE GUARDED

While many men are sexually open, their hearts are often extremely guarded. Conversely, though a man is extremely loving, he may be shut down sexually. Both of these types of men have difficulty connecting the heart and the genitals. For them, love and sex are entirely separate entities. Love may involve the heart, but sex happens between the legs. Not surprisingly, many men find it easy to enjoy sex in the absence of love. If you don't think so, just reflect on their fondness for pornography, masturbation, prostitution, and one-night stands.

THE LIMITATION OF SEX WITHOUT LOVE

The sexual visionary Wilhelm Reich understood the limitation of sex without love. He equated genital sex without a heart connection to pornography. Yet, it's likely that many young men learn about sex as horny teenagers jerking off in the bathroom, devoid of any emotional involvement. Safe in their comfort zones, these young men condition themselves to pursue the shortsighted goal of ejaculation without feeling obliged to love. To make matters worse, their penchant for squandering sexual fluids before the erotic energy has a chance to rise into the heart center further inhibits the possibility of genital–heart connection.

NEWS FLASH: WOMEN ARE MORE LOVING THAN MEN

For most women, sex and love are one: unlike most men, their hearts and genitals are deeply connected. Women intuitively recognize the importance of establishing this kind of deeper connection. For them, it's generally a fairly easy process. When a woman opens herself sexually, the floodgates of her heartfelt emotions, and even her spirituality, may pour forth. Women generally share tantra's viewpoint that love and sex are synonymous. The Hindus use the Sanskrit word "kama," a term that embraces both love and sex indivisibly. Experience tells me that men are more disconnected than women; that's why most men require training in the sexual arts to unify the heart and genitals so that something truly memorable can take place.

MAGNETIC PRINCIPLES AND THE HUMAN BODY

When opposite poles on a magnet meet, strong attraction is created. But did you know that magnetic principles can be applied to the human body? It's true! The vagina is considered the negative pole in the feminine body. The heart center in the middle of her chest is considered a woman's positive pole, including those marvelous extensions, her breasts and nipples.

A man's positive pole is his penis. His negative pole resides in the middle of his chest, the heart center. So when a man and a woman's breasts meet, negative and positive poles are connecting and creating a strong charge. And when a penis and a vagina meet, the same principle holds true. So whenever a man and a woman's opposite poles meet, the potential is there for a perfectly complementary relationship. This is especially true if a circle of energy can be created—but for that to happen, love *must* be present.

AVOID ONE-DIMENSIONAL SEX

Ideally, lovemaking creates a circle of energy. The catch is, love must be present for the heart-genital connection to flow in a circle. Without love, only the sex centers connect. There will be an exchange of energy, but the exchange will be linear—just a straight line that leaves both partners unfulfilled.

One-dimensional sex is like strumming one or two strings of a musical instrument; the instrument's entire spectrum of sounds will never ring out. But if love is present and the heart and genitals meet at their opposite poles, a circle of energy is created. Only then can open hearts truly meet. Only then can two lovers become one. Without the presence of love, deep satisfaction is impossible.

THE HEALING OF EMOTIONAL ISSUES

The core of your ability to feel resides in your heart. Suppressed feelings buried in the heart are like thorns that must be discovered and removed. Without the involvement of the heart, the healing potential of sex is absent. You may achieve intense genital orgasm, but without heartfelt love, you will barely scratch the surface of the range of sexual experiences available to you. The potential for deep healing requires both heart and genitals to be sufficiently open and energetically connected.

Let's be real: sex turns men on. Sex stirs their passion. Men love a genital focus, and they're crazy about women who provide it. You may have noticed that for many men, sex often becomes a barometer for the health of the relationship. The more sex they have, the happier they are in the relationship—but for them, sexual intimacy begins and ends with the genitals and goes no further. So a major dilemma for women is how to hold men to a higher standard of lovemaking that includes the heart as well as the groin.

A HEART-OPENING EXERCISE

The following heart-opening exercise offers men and women a chance to reconcile these seemingly divergent needs. How? By giving him the direct genital stimulation he craves, then helping him channel the energy of arousal upward into his heart center. Raising sexual energy in this fashion connects the heart and the genitals, reuniting love and sex as they were meant to be. In this way, both parties get what they want: the perfect win-win situation. He gratefully receives the genital attention that he craves from her and she becomes the happy recipient of his overflowing heartfelt loving energy.

Let me share this powerful heart-opening exercise with you. It has the potential to activate the heart-genital connection and change the dynamic of your sexual relationship in an extraordinary way. It works equally well for men and women, and may be done solo or with a partner. The directions are simple and are offered here as if you are practicing solo. If you use your imagination, however, this exercise can be easily adapted for partner play.

WHATEVER TURNS YOU ON IS APPROPRIATE

You begin by pleasuring yourself until you achieve arousal. The type of stimuli that you prefer doesn't really matter. Whatever turns you on is fine. Let no man judge! As you allow your arousal to escalate, be prepared to stop before you come. Remember: your game plan is to *avoid* genital release. As you approach orgasm, the traffic light in your head turns red. Cease all stimulation and rest in stillness. While you rest, expand your breathing and bring the focus of your attention to the heart area in the middle of your chest. You'll want to fill the chest cavity with your activated sexual energy, so *imagine* and *feel* the energy of arousal rising into the middle of your chest. Focus your awareness at the chest area for a few minutes. The energy of arousal will ascend. For men, the partial loss of your erection and the hardening of your nipples are clear signs that the sexual energy has been successfully raised. When you've lost about 30 percent of your erection, it is safe to resume stimulation. This cycle can be repeated a half-dozen times or more. This is how you will achieve a marvelous "heart-on."

AVOIDING "BLUE BALLS"

As far as men are concerned, successfully redirecting orgasmic energy to the heart center will prevent the possibility of the painful condition commonly known as "blue balls." This is a condition that used to plague me until I learned to raise sexual energy away from the balls. This peculiar condition arises from prolonged sexual stimulation without a genital release, and without raising orgasmic energy. If the energy of arousal fails to rise, it remains stuck in the prostate gland. This condition involves painful sensations in the testicles accompanied by lower back pain from sore kidneys that may last anywhere from twenty-four to seventy-two hours. Pain like this gives non-ejaculatory sex a bad name. But it was my failure to raise the energy that was the problem, *not* the failure to ejaculate.

In Chinese medicine, the close relationship between the kidneys and sex is well known. Blocked sexual energy equates to sore kidneys, hence, lower back pain. Now that I understand the importance of raising energy, I have eliminated this problem. If you are still having difficulty moving the energy up after prolonged sex play without coming, a firm but gentle massage of the perineum (the area between the anus and genitals) will help disperse "stuck" sexual energy.

KEEP REPEATING THE CYCLE

Each time you successfully raise the energy of arousal to the heart, the pleasuring part of the exercise may be repeated until you once again approach the point of no return. Keep repeating the cycle until there is no more sexual energy to work with or until you just feel like stopping. There is no prohibition against having a climax: just delay it long enough to move as much sexual energy into the heart as you can. My tantra teacher told me to raise the energy and hold back at least seven times. He maintained that if you choose to come at that point, you will not lose vital energy, since the energy has already been successfully transmuted.

HEART-CENTERED ORGASMS CAN BE EMOTIONAL

Heart-centered orgasmic energy is often accompanied by intense emotional releases. Laughing, crying, moans, groans, or other emotional outbursts are not uncommon. Sometimes, the intensity of feeling is so great it eclipses interest in or the need for genital release. Even if you *do* come, you might not even notice your orgasm as it dissolves into the larger drama of the *emotional* climax. Whatever comes up is perfect in the moment. Just stay present and enjoy whatever happens.

THE RESOLUTION OF OLD EMOTIONAL TRAUMAS

Caution: As you learn to direct sexual pleasure into the heart, suppressed feelings from your past are likely to surface. You will then be provided the opportunity to re-experience them. As painful and uncomfortable as that might be, it affords you the opportunity to accept and heal old wounds once and for all. By breathing deeply and committing yourself to the present moment, you can accept, heal, and overcome any old trauma that resurfaces.

Remember that feelings are greatly influenced by the breath. With deep, conscious, abdominal breathing, the source of the suppressed feelings may be touched, moved, and finally resolved. I like to visualize them being redirected back to Mother Earth to be purified and recycled. This is a powerful healing method for releasing suppressed emotional wounds. As you release emotional wounds and past traumas, more of your heart is available for loving both your partner and yourself.

CHAPTER 10

FEMALE SEXUAL SATISFACTION IS VERY IMPORTANT FOR MEN

At this time in our planet's history—a period of so much accelerated change and chaos—it is easy to forget that the importance of female sexual satisfaction only became widely accepted in America during the sexual revolution of the 1960s and the women's movement that accompanied it. And let's not forget that in many parts of the world, and even in certain circles here in the United States, the prevailing attitude toward women's sexuality still centers on a woman's perceived duty to service men at the expense of their own pleasure. Even today, female circumcision (removal of the clitoris) is practiced in some cultures to ensure that women take no pleasure in sex. In ancient China and India, however, sexual pleasure was known to be equally vital to both men and women.

REAL SEXUAL SATISFACTION IS MUTUAL

Tantric teachings remind us that real sexual satisfaction can exist only if it is shared equally between partners. The attitude of tantric lovers toward each other is one of worship. Each sees the other as the embodiment of god or goddess. There is an inherent equality and healthy respect between male and female lovers. They are encouraged to see beyond mundane problems and personality shortcomings, beyond all that might be considered superficial, to honor and recognize the divinity within each other. When you see your lover as a manifestation of divinity, you grow closer to each other—and to your own sense of spirituality.

SERVING THE GODDESS SHOULD BE A MAN'S FOREMOST GOAL

An enlightened man's greatest motivating force is his desire to please his woman. The hunter who excelled during prehistoric times did so because of his desire to appear powerful and virile in the eyes of his woman. Men haven't changed much since then. Today's "hunter" doesn't bring home wild animal skins, but he may indicate his desire for her favor by supplying fine clothes, automobiles, flowers, jewelry, and other forms of material wealth that will tickle her fancy.

MEN MUST LEARN TO HUMBLE THEMSELVES

The ancient teachings are quite clear: to create consistent and harmonious relationships, men must open their hearts and learn to approach sex as a mystical and spiritual act. The challenge for men is to find that "spark of divinity" that they can achieve only through union with the "sacred feminine." Ultimately, they must make love with the attitude that *serving* women is the first and foremost goal. Tantric tradition is quite clear: it is mandatory that women be honored. This includes mother, sister, daughter, wife and grandmother—*all* women. Let's not forget that it is women who give birth and women who nourish. If only men could learn to humble themselves and commit to serving women, the battle of the sexes would end abruptly.

TANTRIC WOMEN HAVE ALWAYS BEEN FULLY EMANCIPATED

Contrary to Judeo-Christian tradition, tantric women have always been fully emancipated. They have always been viewed as initiatresses into the sexual mysteries. Yes, you read that correctly. Women were the *instigators* of sexual interaction. Women have served as priestesses, and have been worshipped as the living goddess. *Tantra* originally evolved in matriarchal societies. Women controlled the economy, the family, and their own bodies. In tantric sexual rites, women have always been accorded the "first rite" of sexual satisfaction. The ancient sages taught that it behooved a man to rouse his lover to as many orgasms as she desired, since a woman's orgasms were as important to the man as to the woman. Her orgasms greatly benefit him by heightening the potency of her female sexual essence. After all, he gets to absorb her powerful feminine energy and the sexual essence that emanates from her through the head of his penis and the membranes of its skin.

SHE ABSORBS THE HEALING HOT MALE ESSENCE

The woman benefits because the involuntary vaginal contractions that accompany her own orgasms serve as the physical mechanism enabling her to absorb the beneficial hot, male essence (not semen) from her partner; this is precisely what she finds so powerful and invigorating. The heightened energy exchange of male/female essences is a nonphysical, yet powerful, health-giving ingredient that serves as a major bonding mechanism. With every additional orgasmic contraction she experiences, her essence achieves greater and greater potency as she draws more rejuvenating male energy into her. Exchanging sexual essence is a means of sharing life-giving energy that was known by the wisdom teachers to be more potent than any food, herb, or medicine.

PROLONGED LEISURELY SEXUAL INTERCOURSE IS IDEAL

The ancient masters were clear that the ideal was to prolong intercourse for as long as possible. The longer the man remained inside the woman, the more sexual essence was exchanged. Of course, there would be no strengthening of his sexual essence if he squandered it by ejaculating. By now, I'm sure you can see that a formidable obstacle to male/female satisfaction is the shortsighted male preference for ejaculation.

HER SATISFACTION IS HIS TOP PRIORITY

When a man makes a woman's sexual satisfaction his top priority, his deeper satisfaction is assured as she opens to him more fully. He becomes the catalyst for her womanhood, and this is what activates and excites his powerful masculine energies. When she is highly aroused and properly satisfied, he is automatically satisfied by the magnetism of her female energy. His is an automatic electric response to her awesome magnetic qualities. Many men agree that there is nothing more erotic than his partner's emerging passion. The more turned-on a woman allows herself to become, the more awakened his male energy gets. Ironically, a woman's greatest opportunity to satisfy a man in sex is in teaching him to successfully fulfill her. Conscious men are smart enough to understand the universal law of energy: whatever you project, you get back. Send her an abundance of love, attention, and sexual pleasure, and she will receive it and return it to you a thousand times over.

CHAPTER 11

THE CHAKRA SYSTEM

While describing the benefits of non-ejaculatory sex for men, I touched briefly upon the strategy of raising orgasmic energy. Let me be clear: once you've mastered seminal retention, the next step in your sexual evolution is directing sexual pleasure upward. Raising sexual energy is an alchemical refinement process that has been known to alter your perceptual reality, and even the way you feel and behave. When you raise sexual energy, your escalating arousal is accompanied by feelings of empowerment, open-heartedness, heightened awareness, and deeper communication. It may even include spiritual revelations. In truth, the failure to direct your sexual energy upward is a failure to fulfill your deepest human potential. All the great traditions of sacred sexuality encourage the raising of orgasmic energy. The ultimate purpose of raising energy is to accelerate the evolution of human consciousness.

In his book, *Taoist Secrets of Love: Cultivating Male Sexual Energy*, Mantak Chia writes:

"The Chinese legends speak of a golden age when all men lived in harmony with nature and transmuted their seed upward as naturally as you or I breathe. By raising orgasmic energy mankind is capable of a much higher existence than what it now accepts."

THREE WAYS TO RESPOND TO SEXUAL AROUSAL

Now, I realize that until you have a basic intellectual understanding of the chakra system, you can't really appreciate the wisdom of *raising* sexual energy. So, let's demystify the process! There are only *three* possible ways you can respond to sexual arousal: First, you can *repress* the sexual urge like many followers of the various religious traditions of the world choose to do. But, trust me, repression is *never* a good idea. It's artificial, unnatural, and contrived. It is certainly not a suitable practice for a health-minded individual. A second and healthier way of responding to arousal is to find a suitable way to *express* it, as I presume most of you are apt to do. Whatever form your sexual expression takes, it may be helpful to think of it as *indulgence* with awareness. In other words, it's not *what* you do; it's how conscious you are as you express yourself. Finally, the third possible way to respond to sexual arousal is to *transform* sexual energy. Tantra is for transformation, which happens when you *raise* orgasmic energy into the higher chakras (the heart and brain). The upward movement of sexual pleasure becomes a blueprint for accessing the mystical (spiritual) world of sex. Physically, it sets the stage for multiple, full-body orgasms and ecstatic sex.

TANTRIC PHILOSOPHY: THE SEVEN SPINAL CHAKRAS

The chakra system comes straight out of tantric philosophy. While you have many chakras, I am going to talk about the seven spinal chakras that are energetically connected to the physical body. In English, *chakras* are energy centers called "vortexes," but in Sanskrit, chakras mean "wheels of light." Light refers to the unseen energy field that surrounds and permeates all life forms, including you and me, your houseplants, and the family dog.

Clairvoyants see chakras as spinning whirlpools of energy located along the spine. As part of the subtle energy system, they are invisible to most of us, but nevertheless quite real. Each chakra has a different rate of vibration or frequency. The fastest is at the crown of the head, while the others vibrate progressively slower. They function a bit like transformers, slowing down cosmic energy as it moves down the chakra "ladder" from the top of the head to the base of the spine. When the vibration frequency pattern of each chakra is operating optimally, you will experience extraordinary health and vitality, enjoy a strong mental focus, and feel a more powerful connection to the wisdom of the heart—and all of creation.

LEARN THE LOCATION OF EACH CHAKRA

Each spinal chakra is connected to and governs the activity of one of the seven endocrine glands in the physical body. The first chakra is located at the base of the spine, and its physical counterparts are the adrenal glands. The second chakra is located at the sacrum, and its physical counterparts are the sex glands. This is the sex chakra. The third chakra is located in the solar plexus area, and its physical counterpart is the pancreas. The fourth chakra is located in the heart center, and its physical counterpart is the thymus gland. The fifth chakra is located at the throat, and its physical counterpart is the thyroid gland. The sixth chakra is located at the third eye (the space between the eyebrows), and its physical counterpart is the pituitary gland. Finally, the seventh chakra is located at the crown of the head, and its physical counterpart is the pineal gland.

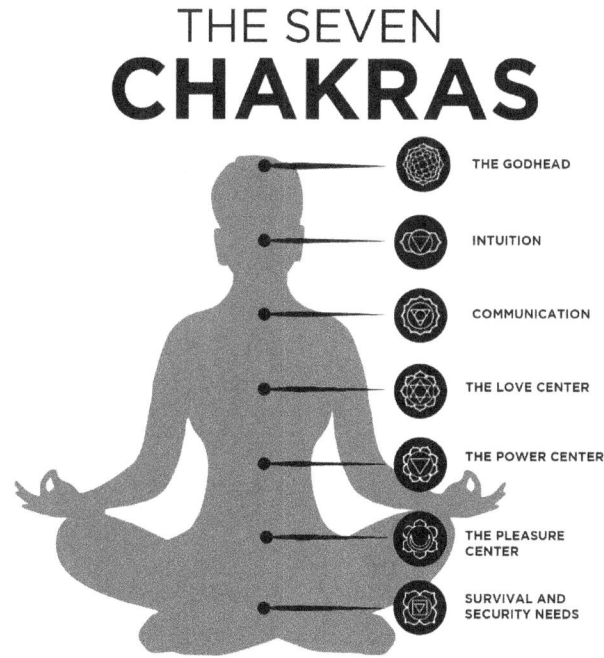

CHAKRAS RESPOND TO EROTIC STIMULATION

Chakras function a bit like erogenous zones. They are sensitive to touch, sound, movement, expanded breathing, and erotic stimulation. During sexual arousal, as the sex chakra responds to the intensity of sexual excitement, it naturally accelerates its vibration frequency pattern. This effectively energizes the sex glands. The sex glands respond by sparking and fueling the rest of the endocrine glands with powerful hormonal secretions. The ability to fire up the sexual apparatus and feed and nourish the rest of the endocrine glands with potent hormonal secretions earns the sex glands the nickname "the stove."

PAY HOMAGE TO EACH CHAKRA

Accomplished lovers not only make it their business to know where each chakra resides, but they pay attentive homage to each one as a way of optimizing their partner's pleasure. For example, if I'm having sex with my partner, I never fail to physically acknowledge the various locations where each chakra resides. This involves applying conscious touches from the tailbone at the base of the spine right on up to the crown of the head. I mentioned earlier that becoming a great lover requires an increase in body awareness, breath awareness, and energy awareness—well, *chakra* awareness is an important link in this chain. For conscious people, lovemaking, like life itself, is one big game of expanded awareness. Life's winners constantly strive to increase awareness in order to facilitate personal growth.

FEED THE STOVE

As you might imagine, sex-positive lovers enjoy feeding the stove (the sex glands) plenty of fuel in the form of erotic stimulation. Students of the sexual arts enjoy the process of keeping the stove fired-up, aroused, and secreting their precious, rejuvenating hormonal cocktails. Amazingly, these hormones not only help us to become conscious, but they also regulate all of the body's functions, including aging, sexuality, and even spirituality. Think of hormones as powerful chemical messengers that can keep you young, expand your view of reality, and regulate your behavior and your mood.

THE SEXUAL ENERGY CYCLE: STAGE ONE

Now let's discuss the *sexual energy cycle*. In order to understand the dynamic connection between ecstatic sex and spirit, the sexual energy cycle must be thoroughly understood. It has two stages. Unfortunately, however, conventional sex includes only the *first* stage of the cycle, since male ejaculation and female climax invariably short-circuit the process, preventing your sexual play from becoming truly *transformational*.

We've all heard that sex begins in the brain—and this is true! Sexual arousal in its myriad forms impacts your brain. Your brain responds by activating your sex glands, initiating the release of the powerful hormones I've discussed. However, the descending movement of energy from the brain to the sexual apparatus completes only *half* of this circular path. As I've said again and again, one of the main shortcomings of ordinary sex is that your climax short-circuits the journey of arousal, thus terminating the sexual energy cycle prematurely.

SEXUAL ENERGY CYCLE: STAGE TWO

The second stage of the cycle is the key to spiritual illumination, since it returns the rejuvenating sexual energy back to its original source: the brain. To complete the second stage, you must *raise* orgasmic energy, thus fulfilling the primary concerns of all the great traditions of sacred sex. As the energy of arousal ascends, the higher chakras are *invigorated*. During this process, the transmutation of sexual energy alters your perception of reality. Here's how: in ordinary reality, as an individual, you are predisposed to see existence as a multiplicity of separate things, and you experience yourself as a separate entity from the rest of the world. But by raising sexual energy and activating the higher chakras, the elegant feeling of oneness that the great spiritual teachers (and more recently modern physicists) speak of tends to emerge.

CONSCIOUSNESS IS TRANSFORMED IN THE BRAIN

Ultimately, this remarkable process facilitates the experience of *interconnectedness* with "All That Is." As sexual energy is returned to the brain, consciousness is transformed. This action precipitates an expanded view of reality that is associated with profound inner peace, happiness, intense creativity, and deep spiritual connection. In this state, a lover may experience the cosmic view of reality, namely *"unity consciousness,"* or the experience of merging with the divine. Unfortunately, for many of you, the realization of unity or oneness remains just a fuzzy intellectual concept. Prolonging your orgasms, however, will provide you with a perfect vehicle for a life-changing, direct experience of this spiritual truth. Be prepared and remain open for what is still to come.

THE FIRST CHAKRA: SURVIVAL AND SECURITY NEEDS

Now, let's have a brief look at each individual chakra as it pertains to sexual energy. The first chakra is known as the root chakra. It is the foundation of the whole chakra system. It is located at the base of the spine between the small triangular bone known as the coccyx, or tailbone, and the pelvic floor that lies between the anus and the genitals. When you perform sexercises, you are strengthening your first chakra.

Each chakra represents a different level of consciousness that attempts to explain human behavior as it is seen from that level. For example, the root chakra deals with basic survival and security needs. Survival needs can be thought of as everything from a mother's breast milk to food, shelter, money, and the need to connect with your tribe. This chakra connects you to Mother Earth and offers you the grounding energy (roots) that is needed to balance the spiritual energies (wings) of the higher chakras.

Sexually speaking, the root chakra puts out a powerful, lusty sex drive that I like to think of as the "energy of aliveness." This powerful *primal* energy represents the life force in your body.

THE SECOND CHAKRA: THE PLEASURE CENTER

The second chakra is located in the lower abdomen, centered between the navel and the genitals in the area of the sacrum. Sometimes called the pleasure center, or the sex center, this chakra deals with your instinct for sexual expression. Sexual behavior is an avenue of self-expression; it's how you relate sexually to the world around you. Sexuality—and all your attitudes toward it—are patterned in this chakra. Sexuality connects you to your own body's physical needs and the potential for exploring your erotic and sensual nature. Explored without shame, erotic energy can elevate the human body and spirit into sensations of ecstasy and higher states of consciousness. On the dark side, sex has been misused as a vehicle for exploitation, abuse, disempowerment, addiction, and control. Negative attitudes toward sex range from embarrassment, shame, and guilt to gluttony and obsession. The Freudian view of human nature sees life primarily from this level of consciousness.

THE THIRD CHAKRA: THE POWER CENTER

The third major energy vortex is known as the solar plexus chakra, or power center. It is located above the navel and below the chest cavity. This center is associated with power issues and emotional feelings, such as self-esteem and self-worth. Conscious sex is very much about empowering your partner. It's a little-known secret that one of the best times to empower a lover with potent affirmations for the express purpose of healing self-esteem issues is just before, during, or immediately after orgasm. This is when the chakras are functioning in a heightened state and the subconscious mind is available for reprogramming. This secret is the basis for many "sex-magic" healing rituals.

THE FOURTH CHAKRA: THE LOVE CENTER

The fourth vortex, the heart chakra, is located in the center of the chest. While your money, sex, and power issues emanate from the lower three chakras, if the heart chakra is open and vibrating at a proper frequency, you can summon the experience of universal love, devotion, compassion, and forgiveness. With the opening of the heart, ego boundaries begin to dissolve, and there is an emerging desire for solidarity with the world. Unconditional love is possible at this level of consciousness. On a sexual level, this is where you direct orgasmic energy to awaken the heart-genital connection. Be aware, though, that the heart area is often heavily guarded due to past emotional traumas. Not until you heal your emotional scars can you expect to experience the optimum flow of the joyful, loving energy that is potentially available.

THE FIFTH CHAKRA: COMMUNICATION

The fifth energy vortex, the throat chakra, is located in the center of the neck. This is where dynamic communication takes place. It deals with creativity, self-expression, and the awesome ability to speak your truth. During uninhibited sexual encounters, moans, groans, laughing, crying, screams, animal noises, and other primal sounds are emitted as a natural form of self-expression, and a way of raising sexual energy into the throat area. As you might imagine, it's important for the energy pathways to remain clear for directing sexual energy upward, so conscious lovers must learn to release muscular tension in their shoulders and neck. Tension inhibits orgasmic flow, and this chakra is where blocked energy often resides. Chronic tension in the shoulders, neck, and throat area is all too common and prevents the orgasmic flow from reaching its final destination, the spiritual faculties in the brain.

THE SIXTH CHAKRA: INTUITION (THE THIRD EYE)

The sixth vortex, the brow chakra or the third eye, is located at the center of the forehead between the eyebrows. This is the center of *intuition*, what is known as the mind's "inner eye." Through this chakra you receive flashes of insight, for this is the center of the brain's psychic abilities. When this center is activated, extra-sensory perception becomes possible, and you experience life from a broader cosmic perspective called "universal mind." From this vantage point, you see things as they really are without the filter of the self, and you recognize the inescapable unity of existence. Conscious sex practices target the brain, since the spiritual faculties reside there. Successfully raising the energy of arousal into the head is an entry point into the mystical world of sex, where your view of reality begins to expand in a profound way.

THE SEVENTH CHAKRA: THE GODHEAD

The seventh and highest major vortex, the crown chakra, is located at the top of the head. This chakra is your link to the divine: to inspiration, guidance, wisdom, and knowledge far higher than your own. This chakra is the center of cosmic consciousness. All spiritual seekers attempt to connect with this center. Its physical counterpart is the brain, with millions of dormant neurons existing as a core of potential just waiting to be activated. As you gain mastery in your ability to direct orgasmic energy to the brain, intuitive knowledge and spiritual powers increase as brain cells blossom like flowering lotus petals.

Now you can better understand why conscious sexual practices always direct orgasmic energy upward toward the light. Not only is the sexual energy refined and transformed on its upward, alchemical journey, but the way you perceive energy also changes. As your view of reality shifts, you get to experience the expanded mystical states common to prolonged, ecstatic lovemaking. As I've already mentioned, the process culminates with the life-altering realization that God is within, and all of existence is interconnected. Subsequently, you are called upon to reject who you thought you were (your body, your mind), in favor of what you now know yourself to be: pure consciousness.

CHAPTER 12

USING BREATH CONTROL TO AVOID MALE EJACULATION

Now that we've covered the less-than-favorable coitus interruptus withdrawal method, the use of direct pressure on the prostate point, and sex muscle control for preventing male ejaculation, there is a fourth method that I would like to share with you that surpasses all the others. But I must warn you: unless you have been exposed to the transformational power of breath-work, you may underestimate the importance of conscious breathing as it applies to lovemaking, and that would be a huge mistake.

THE WAY YOU BREATHE DETERMINES YOUR SEXUAL EXPERIENCE

Most untrained men and women still don't realize that the way you breathe determines the quality and duration of your lovemaking. Let me get straight to the point: yogic breathing, when artfully done, *can* prevent premature male ejaculation. Here's why: Breathing is a rhythmic extension of your nervous system. Depending on how you breathe, you can either stimulate your nervous system or calm it down. In other words, the rate of your breath controls the degree of sexual arousal—ultimately determining if and when a man will ejaculate. A fast, shallow, panting breath tends to over-stimulate. It promotes an increase in heart rate, blood pressure, fear hormones, muscle tension, and excitement, none of which are compatible with ecstatic lovemaking.

ABDOMINAL BREATHING PROMOTES RELAXATION

On the other hand, abdominal breathing—the kind that you learn in yoga class—promotes relaxation, calmness, and a sense of wellbeing.

By bringing the parasympathetic nervous system into play, it inhibits the urge to ejaculate. Abdominal breathing initiates a relaxation response that slows down your brainwaves from their normal frantic pulse to a much calmer, more meditative pace. This relaxation response is perfectly compatible with prolonged, leisurely lovemaking that leads to ecstatic sex. Conscious breathing that begins in the belly and includes the chest is a man's best strategy for mastering seminal retention, and it also provides the foundation for amazing implosive orgasms.

DEEPEN AND SLOW THE BREATH

The average person breathes about fifteen times per minute, but the rate of breathing that induces the relaxation response is eight breaths per minute—so practice slowing down your breathing as you would in a yoga class, or in meditation. Breath control is a huge part of conscious sexuality, facilitating extended lovemaking, expanded awareness, and spiritual progress.

YOUR ABILITY TO BREATHE MAY BE COMPROMISED

Although breathing is a natural function, many of you use only a fraction of your breathing potential. Your ability to breathe fully may get compromised in the womb, at birth, during infancy, or later. Though your fully expanded lungs hold about seven pints of air, many of you take in less than *one* pint per breath. In short: *many of you are barely breathing*. It's hardly any wonder that you sometimes feel only half alive! Stress, chronic muscular tension, devitalized foods, negative emotions, poor posture, air and water pollution, and toxic lifestyles all contribute to alterations in your natural breathing patterns, resulting in shallow or irregular breathing.

BREATHE LIKE A SLEEPING BABY

Though breathing comes naturally, many of you have forgotten the most natural way to breathe. If you want to know what natural breathing looks like, just observe a healthy, sleeping baby. You'll notice that the inhaled breath is through the nose. The breath first fills the abdomen, and then expands into the chest. There is a slight pause. On the exhaled breath, the belly pulls in toward the spine as the breath is released. Once again, there is a pause between breaths, but now the pause is longer before the breath returns and the cycle is repeated.

One of the reasons I recommend yoga and meditation to all my students is so they can practice the art of natural breathing until mastery is achieved.

BREATHE FROM THE BELLY AND THE CHEST

Close your eyes for a moment and focus on the way you naturally breathe. Do it right now! You may observe that your breathing is shallow and frequent. For some of you, the breath may reach only into the chest, never moving the belly at all. For others, the breath may reach the belly, but not move up into the chest. The point is this: if you're not breathing fully, you're not living fully. To breathe only into the upper chest is to avoid the powerful creative energies of the lower belly and sexual organs. To breathe only into the belly is to avoid the equally strong creative energies of the heart and throat. The balance, obviously, is found in activating both "breath centers" simultaneously.

PROPER BREATHING WILL CONTROL SEXUAL EXCITEMENT

Employing complete breathing is the perfect antidote to sexual tension. Proper breathing will assist you in gaining control over sexual excitement by promoting relaxation and calmness. Skillful lovers use their breath like a precision instrument, revving up the system to generate sexual energy and excitement or toning it down as needed. My yoga teacher always encouraged me to imagine myself breathing with my whole body. I have found this tip to be very helpful for circulating sexual energy throughout the body.

DEEP BREATHING WILL EXPAND YOUR ORGASMIC CAPACITY

Expanded breathing is the driving force for circulating sexual energy. Deep breathing will not only expand your orgasmic capacity, but it will increase your capacity for feeling alive. If you think about it, ecstatic sexual energy is the energy of aliveness. With expanded breathing, you can learn to feel sexual energy running through all your cells, not just your genitals. I've already mentioned that the breath propels the energy of feeling. This is one of the secrets to initiating multiple full-body orgasms. Though every cell is potentially orgasmic, three things must happen in order to realize this incredible potential. First, you must hover just below the genital release point, on the cutting-edge of orgasm for an extended period. Second, you must avoid coming. And finally, the sexual charge must be sufficiently circulated by the breath to activate the cellular structures of the head and feet and all the spaces in between. Breathe, baby, breathe!

COMBINING BREATH AWARENESS AND MOVEMENT

In my role as a tantric instructor, I have often been called upon to assist men in their lovemaking. In a typical introductory session, I have the men lie down on a massage table as I instruct them in proper breathing. If they prove adept at breathing, they are ready to engage with my female partner. She manually stimulates them to peak arousal. As their orgasm coach, I encourage the men to breathe fully from the belly and the chest. The emphasis is on relaxation. The men are reminded not to create any unnecessary tension in their body. That means keeping the body soft. If the men become too hot, we stop until they cool down and the danger of coming has passed. This cycle is repeated throughout a typical hour-long session. If the man has shown that he has mastered the art of complete breathing, and he is successful at avoiding a genital release, he is ready to apply his newfound breathing success with his sexual partner, if he has one. If not, he can practice solo.

If he has a partner, I devise a game plan for his next lovemaking session. Typically, I ask that he coordinate each of his pelvic thrusts with a conscious out-breath as a means of staying present and cool in the heat of arousal. For example, upon penetration, I ask that he exhale deeply as he thrusts forward into his partner's sacred space. After waiting patiently for the breath to return, I encourage him to take a long, slow, comfortable inhale upon near withdrawal from his partner's vagina. This is followed by another exhale coordinated with another forward thrust deep inside. The idea is to coordinate every pelvic thrust, both in and out, with the breath. I encourage him to maintain that rhythmic sequence throughout the entire lovemaking session. Successful breathing equals staying power!

STOP HURRYING THROUGH SEX

It takes quite a bit of focus and discipline to succeed in this scenario, especially with a passionate partner, but it is well worth the effort. Due to the slow pacing of the deep breathing, the lovemaking takes on the added depth and calm focus of a moving meditation. Slowing down your pelvic thrusts to match the rhythm of the breath effectively neutralizes a man's tendency to hurry through sex. Ecstatic sex needs time —the longer, the better. The additional time ensures that the awakened energy will penetrate deeper into your being. With more time, the orgasmic energy will spread from the toes to the head—every fiber of your body will be throbbing with it.

If, however, you are in a hurry, the awesome implosive orgasm that can thrill you from corner to corner and end to end becomes just an ejaculation, almost meaningless. You will feel tired, frustrated, and let down because the energy is lost. To negate that possibility, the slow, methodical rhythm of deep breathing forces men to slow down and remain cool. Unhurried sex is your ticket to ecstatic lovemaking. It will satisfy any man or woman. Of course, this scenario works best when both partners coordinate their breathing to match each other's rhythm.

BREATHING WITH A PARTNER

Let me share two different breathing techniques that can be employed when working with a partner. Using what is called the "harmonizing breath," the couple does everything together: they inhale together, pause between each breath together, exhale together, and pause together again. The second breathing technique is known as the "reciprocal charging breath." This time, one partner breathes in as the other partner breathes out, and they continue in that fashion throughout the entirety of their lovemaking.

Have fun with it. The idea is to remain conscious of the energy your partner is sending you as well as the energy you are sending back. It's not so much which style of breathing you choose to use—

rather, it's more about how conscious you are with each breath and your ability to stay present. Expanded breathing will orient your lovemaking toward energy exchange, shared affection, and nurturance. Shallow breathing, on the other hand, typically results in energy loss, fatigue, and disappointment.

EYE GAZING: A SOUL CONNECTION WITH YOUR PARTNER

Conscious breathing is an advanced technique. When combined with eye gazing, an ancient technique that facilitates intimacy, it can be quite erotic. Gazing into the eyes of another human being is an intimate experience that can establish a profound connection at the soul level. The technique requires a softening of the eyes, a steady gaze, and the ability to stay in the here and now. Of course, the flip side is allowing yourself to be seen. Eye gazing works best when you objectively observe any thoughts, feelings, or physical sensations that might arise without making any judgments about what you see or experience. Be curious, but detached. Make no attempt to change anything; instead, just watch the process unfold as though you were watching a movie.

EYE GAZING MAY BECOME TRANCE-LIKE

Quite often, I simply lie down with my partner. We rest on our sides, facing each other, and connect with a gaze as we breathe together. As a variation, we perform a tantric exercise whereby we imagine and feel the left eye receiving love and the right eye sending love. It works like this: upon inhaling I receive love through the left eye, and while exhaling I send love through the right eye. After a few minutes of strong focus, it's not unusual for the image of my partner to begin "shape-shifting"—in other words, the exercise becomes trance-like. The key is to simply be present with what is happening, and not attached to the outcome. About 80 percent of your attention should be with yourself, and 20 percent with the other person. This is a marvelous way to connect with a partner before sex or whenever sexual intimacy seems appropriate.

This simple exercise can become a memorable experience. It can result in feeling more intimate and united with your partner, both erotically and spiritually. In my experience, many women long for sexual intimacy of this type. This is a great way to deepen your connection with your partner.

MAKE BREATH AWARENESS A DAILY PRACTICE

Some of you may still be skeptical about the importance of breath awareness, since breathing is such an automatic process and it's so easy to take for granted. If you are like most people, especially if you haven't taken yoga classes or learned to meditate, chances are that you are completely unconscious of your breath. I totally get it. After all, breathing just continues on its own. All you need to do to continue breathing is *exist*. But, unlike other automatic processes, such as the circulation of blood or the digestion of food, it's possible for anyone to consciously influence and control the flow of breath. It just takes increased breath awareness and daily practice.

SHALLOW BREATHING PROTECTS YOU FROM PAIN

Breath training can be quite challenging, since many of you mastered shallow breathing as infants. Defenseless and dependent as you were, shallow breathing was a handy mechanism to protect yourself from feeling the full depth of your pain and frustration. It still offers you protection in that way, but the downside is that it suppresses your ability to feel pleasure. In other words, if you don't have the presence of mind to expand your breathing in order to fully feel the so-called "negative emotions" (shame, fear, sadness, anger, and grief), then you may forfeit the opportunity to fully experience intense sexual pleasure and joyful exuberance.

SHALLOW BREATHING INITIATES THE FIGHT OR FLIGHT REFLEX

Shallow breathing switches on the sympathetic nervous system. This is the part of your nervous system that is associated with your fight-or-flight reflex; it's a species-wide survival mechanism. When your breath pattern is shallow and rapid, the body assumes you are in danger. This may be an appropriate response when your life is being threatened, but certainly not when you are making love. Shallow breathing during sex creates a condition where the body needlessly undergoes the stress of being on alert and finds itself responding to an imagined crisis. When shallow breathing becomes habitual, it can lead to sexual problems, chronic fatigue, and weakness. Learning to turn off this emergency system when it isn't needed is vital to good sex *and* good health.

PREMATURE EJACULATORS ARE SHALLOW BREATHERS

Sexually speaking, there is a direct cause and effect relationship between shallow breathing and the ability to generate and contain sexual energy. Premature ejaculators and men who experience some degree of erectile dysfunction are invariably shallow breathers. Many women who fail to orgasm are also shallow breathers. For years, I have observed that even during orgasm some lovers restrict their breathing, at times holding their breath completely, thus sabotaging a potentially ecstatic experience. It bears repeating: the movement of sexual energy in the body is propelled by the breath. Generating and containing a strong sexual charge requires expanded breathing. With some breath training, pleasurable feelings can be amplified and many sexual problems can be overcome.

CONSCIOUS BREATHING AND THE POWER OF NOW

On a spiritual level, the breath is the focus that takes you into higher levels of experience. Remember that expanded breathing enhances aliveness. Breath awareness is one way to achieve total presence in the here and now! When you are fully present, you will have transcended mind. When you transcend mind there are no thoughts: you have risen above thought. You may recall that the absence of thought is known as a *no mind* state. In a no mind state there is no past or future. You are anchored fully in the present moment. Yes, conscious breathing is a key to experiencing "the power of now."

THE FOUNDATION OF CONSCIOUS SEX

The inability to stay in the present moment is one of the major barriers to dynamic sex. In yogic circles, breath awareness has always been an anchor into the present moment. Too many untrained men ignore this moment. They let their mind wander, and some even fantasize during sex. The Taoists call this "mating with ghosts." But those of you who meditate on the breath know that conscious breathing is the key to staying present; it prevents you from getting lost in the labyrinth of the mind. The mind with its incessant thinking is like a torrent of aggressive rats, so it's helpful to use the breath as a tool to transcend mind. If I could just take one thing in my "medicine bag" to assist people in the process of transformation or healing—if I had to throw away all my other tools, everything else I know—it would be conscious breathing.

I once interviewed Lana Clarke, a longtime *tantra* teacher. Referring to her experience with a former lover, Lana had this to say about the breath:

"We had an intense experience of tantra. All we did was breathe. We never needed other techniques. There was a natural emphasis on breath. We didn't say, Okay, now let's breathe together. We were so naturally in synch with our breathing that it seemed as though we shared the same breath. When I looked at him across the room, we inhaled together, and it was the same breath. It's like I saw my body breathing him. I saw breath being breathed by God. When I looked back after our relationship was over and I asked myself, what do I miss? What is this intense longing? It wasn't the sex, which was fantastic: it was breathing with him, because that always led me to the awareness of the god/goddess within."

A BREATHING MEDITATION FOR YOU

Let's practice a few rounds of complete breathing. This exercise may be done sitting, standing, or lying down. Breathe through your nose: the mouth is for eating, the nose for breathing. Focus your attention on your lower abdomen. On the in breath, the belly puffs up like a balloon and the chest rises slightly as the lungs fill. Retain the breath for one count. On the out breath, the belly pulls in towards the spine as the lungs empty. Notice the pause between each breath and wait patiently for the breath to return. Let each inhale be long, slow, and comfortable. Let each exhale be more relaxed than the one before it. You are receiving energy with every in-breath. You are relaxing and letting go of tension and stress with every out-breath. Each time you become aware that the mind has wandered, bring the mind back to a concentrated focus on the breath. Continue in this fashion for at least five minutes. This is the natural way to breathe.

Find time each day to practice complete breathing until it becomes natural. Correct breathing will enliven your body, mind, and spirit. Enjoy the journey!

CHAPTER 13

THE FEMININE VERSION OF SEX: SOFT STYLE

Here's a meditative style of lovemaking that can assist in *prolonging* sexual intercourse and delaying, or preventing, unwanted male genital release. This is another advanced method of ejaculation control that seasoned meditators will have a special affinity for, since it mimics the foundational principles of meditation. Like the other methods of prevention, it is best employed just before the point of no return. Approaching the point of peak arousal, you relay a pre-arranged signal to your partner so that she refrains from further stimulation. Since you are already in a high state of arousal, any additional stimulation at this time is counterproductive.

HONOR THE GAME PLAN

Since the game plan is to prolong coitus, the moment of ejaculation inevitability must be avoided. As the arousal escalates and the release point is in sight, be like a driver approaching a yellow traffic light. Slow down and proceed with caution! You know from past experience that in a few seconds the traffic light will turn red, and that's the time to be still and meditate. In stillness, the only movement is the movement of the breath. It is said that tantra brings meditation to sex, and sex to meditation. Now this concept comes mightily into play.

Here's how it plays out: Assume a comfortable position and begin synchronized breathing with your partner. Stay present! In stillness, scan your body and release tension wherever you find it by breathing deeply into the problem area. Do not tighten up! Keep the body soft. Continue relaxing and letting go with each out-breath. Make sure your anus and genitals stay relaxed throughout the process. As you deepen your relaxation, you are diffusing sexual tension and promoting the flow of energy throughout the body. You are meditating in sexual union with your partner! The emphasis is on shared affection and heightened awareness. Soft-style lovemaking is the feminine version of intercourse.

LET THE BODY SOFTEN

Soft-style sex is the antithesis of conventional friction sex. There are no thrusting movements and pumping pelvises. No great athletic feats are required. In soft style sex, you don't chase sexual pleasure. You don't chase orgasm! There is no performance goal, and therefore no fear of underperforming. Instead, you *retreat* from peak arousal and rest in the throes of the *valley orgasm*. In the valley, you use your awareness to direct the energy of arousal away from the genitals and let it stream throughout the rest of the body. This is an "effortless effort." Let the body soften like butter melting in the sun. No voluntary movement of any kind is needed, though the body may move involuntarily of its own accord. If the body wants to move of its own accord, do not resist! Let the wisdom of the body do its thing!

SURRENDER ALL EFFORTS

Friction sex is an extremely masculine form of lovemaking. The tendency is for it to be hard, fast, and athletic. As such, the role reversal in soft-style lovemaking can be particularly effective in harmonizing and balancing masculine and feminine energies. Alternating the roles of giving and receiving, being active and passive, moving and then resting in stillness: these are potent strategies for balancing polar opposites.

Soft-style lovemaking may satisfy a woman's need for physical affection in ways that friction sex cannot. In stillness she has time to tune in physically and emotionally; she can be fully present to enjoy the fruits of leisurely lovemaking. He gets to relax by voluntarily surrendering all physical effort. His receptiveness affords him the opportunity to consciously absorb her luscious feminine energy. Though the couple may appear outwardly motionless, inwardly their energy is dynamic and connected. Conservation of genital orgasm is likely with soft-style sex. When you avoid the futility of striving for orgasm, the energy of arousal can expand and circulate until every cell is turned on. In this scenario, the lovers experience the valley orgasm as total bliss. This type of coupling may continue for a half-hour, an hour, or more. Its timeless quality is not attained by endurance, or even duration, but by deep relaxation and the *absence* of purpose and hurry.

THE LOVERS RADIATE IN BLISSFUL STILLNESS

In stillness, the erotic experience of each lover may become heightened to the point where the sexual union is excruciatingly pleasurable beyond anything they may have experienced in friction sex. As the letting go deepens, orgasmic energy oozes throughout the lover's bodies. Each lover feels their partner's body and the energy that emanates from it flowing toward them, and they merge with that energy. They melt in it!

AWARENESS OF SUBTLE ENERGY

The natural energetic flow between lovers is happening anyway, but the passive/receptive nature of soft-style lovemaking optimizes your ability to become aware of subtle energy. Think of this exchange as a river of energy moving back and forth between partners. If you are in total surrender, a variety of tangible physical sensations may become evident. Throbbing, warmth, tingles, pulsations, shivers, vibrations, and involuntary movements may be felt at various places in the body, or even from head to toe. Do not resist! You are in an altered state!

FRICTION SEX HAS ITS PLACE

Don't misunderstand me—friction sex is not a bad thing, but quite the opposite: it can be perfectly complementary to soft-style sex. The in-and-out pelvic pumping of friction sex is useful for generating excitement and increasing arousal, but the downside is that if a man lacks the necessary awareness and restraint, it will take him over the edge. Additionally, sometimes the aggressive and repetitive nature of friction sex tends to numb or desensitize the genitalia of either sexual partner, especially if the lovemaking is too hard, too fast, or lasts too long. You need a plan B! Meditative, soft-style sex is your plan B.

MEN ARE ELECTRIC, WOMEN ARE MAGNETIC

The challenge for men is that soft-style lovemaking goes against their masculine nature. From an alchemical standpoint, the male is electric while the female is magnetic. It is the nature of electricity to move. For men, the constant motion of friction sex feels natural and defines their masculine style. On the other hand, females love to nest, cuddle and embrace. Soft-style sex will satisfy a woman's craving for sexual intimacy in ways that hard, fast, athletic, friction sex rarely can.

CONSCIOUS MEN MUST ACCESS THEIR FEMININE SIDE

Therefore, it requires a bit of a role reversal for men to succeed in soft-style lovemaking. Men must learn to access their passive, receptive, feminine side in order to make this work. The fact that they are in a high state of arousal makes the task even more daunting. The challenge for the James Bond, action-type of man is in the *non-doing*. It may seem counterintuitive, but he can optimize the benefits of his manliness by accessing his gentler feminine side as he enters into energetic communion with his female partner. This is the perfect time for him to embrace her and give and receive as much heartfelt love and affection as possible.

IT'S A CHANCE FOR A MAN TO SURRENDER CONTROL

Soft-style sex represents a rare chance for men to surrender control in the bedroom. In his utter passivity and receptiveness, he becomes a sponge absorbing the magnetic, loving feminine energies that she will release in the sexual exchange. It's as if the door to her loving inner nature swings open, flooding him with healing and rejuvenating life-force energy. This is a powerful way for men to increase the potency of their sexual energy—which of course, turns women on even more. In my experience women love when a man can access his feminine qualities. It turns them on! As I think about it, virtually every time I've allowed myself to be vulnerable in the presence of a woman she has responded compassionately and even erotically.

RELAX INTO THE VALLEY ORGASM

Soft-style lovemaking will take a man from peak arousal to the valley orgasm—a point where a man does not even need a full erection to experience sexual ecstasy. In stillness, cuddling with his partner, he may lose 30 percent or more of his erection. Who cares? His "soft-off" need *not* be a problem. It's actually an asset, since the head of a soft penis is extremely effective at absorbing her feminine essence through the membranes of its skin. Remember, though, soft-style sex is not genital-focused: ideally, it is an ecstatic, full-body sensory experience. Should an erection be desired, slow, calculated micro-movements—only enough to stay hard—will suffice. Once an erection is attained, and peak arousal is once again approached, it is time for the lovers to *retreat in stillness*, relax, and re-experience another ecstatic valley orgasm.

ARTFUL LOVEMAKING IS LIKE A PLAYFUL, EROTIC DANCE

Artful sex requires the skillful use of polar opposites: masculine and feminine, yin and yang, sexual tension and relaxation, movement and stillness, stimulation and delay, the active and the passive, hard and soft. Each has its rightful place. Conscious lovemaking is very much about feeling comfortable in your body and balancing male and female energies for the most delicious fun. Think of your lovemaking as a playful, erotic dance.

HOMEWORK ASSIGNMENT: If you do not have a partner, keep practicing creative self-pleasuring. Make skillful use of proper breathing and holdbacks that ensure the success of non-ejaculatory sex. If you want to become an accomplished lover, here is your chance to refine your bedroom skills. You are preparing for your next sexual partner.

If you do have a partner, you can practice exploring the skillful use of polar opposites in your lovemaking. Practice expanded breathing throughout your sexual play to heighten the energy exchange with your lover. Use the techniques explored earlier in this book to avoid coming and concentrate on sharing affection. Bring meditation to your sexual play when you need to retreat from peak arousal. Use every exhalation as an opportunity to relax. Practice the art of non-doing together with your partner. Stay fully present, going nowhere, and melt like butter in the sun. If your mind wanders, bring it back. Refocus on your breathing. Get out of your head and into your body. Do not strive for sexual pleasure. Do not strive for anything! Master non-doing! There are no performance goals. Have fun—and be gentle with yourself.

CHAPTER 14

FINAL THOUGHTS

The tantric practice of balancing male and female energies has an important role to play in the evolution of our species and the healing of our culture. Let's face it—this culture lacks gender harmony and equilibrium because the male/female energies are so out of balance. Men seek, and have achieved, physical, political, financial, religious, and intellectual advantage over women. Our patriarchal culture reveres male energy, even to the extent of worshipping a male god. Practically everything favors men! But here's the problem: male dominance is pathological. Toxic masculinity takes many forms: sex without love, the exploitation and the abuse of women, the breakdown of home life, high powered technology without reverence for life (like our insane nuclear arsenal), the pollution of the earth, militarism, poverty, environmental destruction—all display male dominance and contempt for the feminine. Many women struggling for recognition have simply begun to act more male. Regrettably, they've abandoned the power and grace of their unique and awesome feminine energy. This has only made things worse.

WOMEN ARE HELD TO A DIFFERENT SEXUAL STANDARD

Contempt for the feminine is a cultural phenomenon. One blatant example is the double standard as it applies to male sexual behavior. Until now, the common belief has been that men should be allowed to "sow their wild oats," since overwhelming biological urges control them. This unenlightened attitude has freed promiscuous males from condemnation and accountability for their indulgent sexual behavior seemingly forever.

But what the culture has failed to acknowledge is that women experience *strong* biological urges, too. Unlike men, though, women do *not* get a free pass. Instead, they are punished by an unfair, deplorable double standard. Sexually promiscuous women are universally condemned, and they invariably suffer cruel judgment if they choose to express their powerful sexual needs the same way men are permitted to. In our culture, they are commonly branded as sluts and whores, if not worse. In some foreign cultures they are even put to death. This attitude is incredibly unfair. It obviously takes a great amount of self-awareness and self-control to harness the creative power inherent in the sexual force and use it constructively. Many powerful men from all walks of life, even presidents and popes, have failed to keep their sexual urges under control, and yet many of them have escaped societal scrutiny. Why should sexually adventurous women be held to a different standard? It takes proper instruction in the sexual arts, not condemnation and blame, to channel sexual urges in a healthy and constructive way, and in an enlightened culture this applies to men and women equally.

HOLD MEN ACCOUNTABLE

As the awakening women's movement reignites and the feminine energies continue to emerge, I'm sure we'll be seeing more cultural upheaval like the recent *#MeToo* movement that has finally begun to hold powerful men accountable for wretched sexual behavior toward women. The pendulum is continually in motion and will ultimately land in the center. Until then, this spirited women's movement will only grow in intensity until a semblance of balance has been achieved.

IT'S A QUESTION OF BALANCE

That's why I am so excited for you, the reader, to establish sex as a higher act of love by targeting the heart chakra in your sexual play. This game-changing tactic is one of the most pleasurable and effective ways to restore the balance of male/female energies. The world simply needs more loving and compassionate men, and by emphasizing the genital-heart connection in your sexual play you now have a proven method for accelerated change. Of course, you must cultivate your own garden before you can change the world. You must become the change you hope to see in others! As you embrace the challenge of directing sexual pleasure upward, your developing feminine qualities will surely emerge. The awesome heartfelt qualities of love, compassion, forgiveness, devotion, nurturance, and vulnerability will redefine you. Your inevitable transformation will set the stage for a new man: an evolutionary leap for humankind.

TRUE GENIUS

Finding a balance and a union between your own masculine and feminine energies is your ultimate task. A balanced man has refined and developed both energies and can manifest each of them comfortably. He can bring what's most appropriate to each moment. In an emotional moment, he is there to *feel* it. In an intellectual exchange, he is there to *understand* it. Einstein, one of my heroes, provides us with a great role model. I'm convinced he received his "Theory of Relativity" *intuitively* (his feminine side), but he also had the mathematical skill to express it *intellectually* (his masculine side). That is *true* genius! Only when you, too, learn to use each sex's unique energies in tandem and in balance will you feel complete.

TWO TYPES OF READERS

I imagine that there are essentially two types of men that will find themselves drawn to this book. The first type includes those of you on a spiritual path seeking to better integrate sexuality with spiritual growth. You may already accept the premise that sex is an inherently spiritual activity, but until now you've lacked the roadmap for integration. That is no longer the case! You now have the tools to implement a *revolutionary* idea that will update and redefine your purpose, namely, directing orgasmic energy *up*, not *out*. Of course, this requires male restraint (non-ejaculatory sex), raising sexual energy (transformation), and embracing the wonder and magic of *altered states*.

In addition, your manly agenda in the new sexual paradigm includes the recognition that first and foremost your goal in sex is being of service to your female partner. You may recall that in tantric circles she represents the living goddess, so the emphasis is always on her pleasure. For those of you with a sexual healer's mindset and a willing partner, that may include G-spot massage. This female-centric vision is a time-tested formula for harmony in sexual relationships. Men: resist this strategy at your own peril!

THE DOOR IS ALWAYS OPEN

The second type of reader has no interest in spirituality and feels uncomfortable associating it with sexual matters, but you're intrigued by the prospect of *boosting* sexual pleasure. Perhaps you're fascinated with the concept of prolonged orgasm. Maybe you want to sexually satisfy your partner(s) more thoroughly, alleviate sexual frustration, overcome boredom with sex, heal impotency and premature ejaculation, or maybe just take your sex life to the next level.

If this sounds like you and you possess the necessary discipline, the techniques described in this book will bring you the ultimate satisfaction you crave. All it takes is a sincere effort to hone your lovemaking skills. Once you get the sex part down—who knows? You may want to go further and explore the realm of energy and spirit. The choice is always yours—and the door is always open.

A SERIOUS, BUT PLEASURABLE EFFORT

Having traveled this path, I am well aware of the *effort* involved in altering sexual behavior, pleasurable though it may be. Learning sexual secrets is one thing, but using them to transform your spiritual life is quite another. The techniques in this book have been tested and refined by countless lovers over thousands of years. I have merely demystified them as best I can. But the only way to benefit from them is to *use* them.

It's worth reminding you that except for a handful of tantra teachers, virtually no one is teaching the art of sexual ecstasy or its connection to spirit. Unfortunately, this dynamic connection is simply not yet acknowledged by this society. Think about it! When was the last time you even heard a mention of the compelling sexual/spiritual link? Maybe never!

HOLD YOURSELF TO A HIGHER STANDARD

In spite of that grave omission, or perhaps because of it, you may feel called to pursue the study of the sexual mysteries. If so, you will be afforded the opportunity to use the vehicle of ecstatic sex to connect with the unseen, yet powerful spiritual forces that penetrate and surround you. If that's the case, I would encourage you to consider taking up yoga and meditation as an adjunct to the sexual techniques described in this book. These spiritual practices will increase your awareness on many levels. They will provide a strong foundational support that will surely translate to your success as a dynamic lover and a more conscious and loving human being. In the meantime: may this book inspire you to hold yourself to a higher standard in the bedroom and in life, for the greater good of all.

THE END

BIBLIOGRAPHY

PREFACE:

Saraswati, Sunyata, and Bodhi Avinasha. *Jewel in the Lotus: The Sexual Path to Higher Consciousness.* San Francisco: Kriya Jyoti Tantra Society, 1987.

INTRODUCTION:

Masters, William H., and Virginia E. Johnson. *Human Sexual Inadequacy.* Boston: Little, Brown, and Co., 1970.

The San Francisco Examiner, A-11, February 10, 1999.

Heisenberg, Werner. *Physics and Phiosophy*, New York: Harper and Row, 1962.

Stapp, H.P. *S-Matrix Interpretation of Quantum Theory.* Physical Review Vol. D3 March 15, 1971.

Gordon, Richard. *The Polarity Experience: Your Healing Hands.* Unity Press, Santa Cruz, 1978.

CHAPTER 1:

Chia, Mantak. *Taoist Secrets of Love: Cultivating Male Sexual Energy.* New York: Aurora Press, 1984.

Muir, Charles, and Caroline. *Tantra: The Art of Conscious Loving.* San Francisco: Mercury House, 1989.

Masters, William H., and Virginia E. Johnson. *Human Sexual Response.* Boston: Little, Brown, and Co., 1966.

Chang, Jolan. *The Tao of Love and Sex: The Ancient Chinese Way to Ecstasy.* New York: E.P. Dutton, 1977.

Saraswati, Sunyata, and Bodhi Avinasha. *Jewel in the Lotus: The Sexual Path to Higher Consciousness.* San Francisco: Kriya Jyoti Tantra Society, 1987.

Anand, Margo. *The Art of Sexual Ecstasy: The Path of Sacred Sexuality for Western Lovers.* Los Angeles: Jeremy Tarcher, 1989.

Chang, Stephen T., *The Tao of Sexology: The Book of Infinite Wisdom.* San Francisco: Tao Publishing, 1986.

Woods, Margo. *Masturbation Tantra and Self Love.* Published by Mho and Mho Works, 1981.

CHAPTER 2:

Harris, Bill. *Thresholds of the Mind.* Beaverton, OR: Centerpointe Press, 2002.

Heisenberg, Werner. *Physics and Phiosophy*, New York: Harper and Row, 1962.

Stapp, H.P. *S-Matrix Interpretation of Quantum Theory.* Physical Review Vol. D3 March 15, 1971.

CHAPTER 3:

Jong, Erica. *Fear of Flying.* New York: Holt, Rinehart and Winston, 1973.

Chia, Mantak. *Taoists Secrets of Love: Cultivating Male Sexual Energy.* New York: Aurora Press, 1984.

Chang, Jolan. *The Tao of Love and Sex: The Ancient Chinese Way to Ecstasy.* New York: E. P. Dutton, 1977.

CHAPTER 4:

Reich, Wilhelm. *The Function of Orgasm.* Translated by Vincent R. Carfagno. New York: Farrar, Straus and Giroux, 1973.

Rajneesh, Bhagwan Shree (Osho). *The Book: An Introduction to the Teachings of Bhagwan Shree Rajneesh.* Rajneeshpuram, OR:

Rajneesh Foundation International, 1984.

Griscom, Chris. *The Ageless Body.* Santa Fe, NM: Light Institute Press, 1992.

Bubba Free John. *Love of the Two-Armed Form.* The Johannine Daist Communion, 1978.

Chia, Mantak. *Taoists Secrets of Love: Cultivating Male Sexual Energy.* New York: Aurora Press, 1984.

Ramsdale, David Alan, and Ellen Jo Dorfman. *Sexual Energy Ecstasy: A Guide to the Ultimate Sexual Experience.* Playa Del Rey: Peak Skill Publishing, 1985.

CHAPTER 5:

Chia, Mantak. *Taoists Secrets of Love: Cultivating Male Sexual Energy.* New York: Aurora Press, 1984.

Chang, Jolan. *The Tao of Love and Sex: The Ancient Chinese Way to Ecstasy.* New York: E.P. Dutton, 1977.

CHAPTER 6:

Freud, Sigmund, and Ernest Jones. *The International Journal of Psycho-analysis.* London, England: 1969.

Kinsey, Alfred, Wardell B. Pomeroy, and Clyde E. Martin. *Sexual Behavior in the Human Female.* Philadelphia: W. B. Saunders, 1953.

Grafenberg, Ernest. *The Role of the Urethra in Female Orgasm.* The International Journal of Sexology, 1950.

Ladas, Alice Kahn, Beverly Whipple, and John D. Perry. *The G-Spot and Other Recent Discoveries about Human Sexuality.* New York: Holt, Rinehart and Winston, 1982.

Masters, William H., and Virginia E. Johnson. *Anatomy of the Female Orgasm.* The Encyclopedia of Sexual Behavior, edited by Ellis and Abarbanel, New York: 1961.

Perry, John D., and Beverly Whipple. *If Your Sexual Response is Poor, the Cause Could Be Weak PC Muscles.* Forum: The International Journal of Human Relations, 1981.

Anand, Margo. *The Art of Sexual Ecstasy: The Path of Sacred Sexuality for Western Lovers.* Los Angeles: Jeremy P. Tarcher, 1989.

Muir, Charles and Caroline. *Tantra: The Art of Conscious Loving.* San Francisco: Mercury House, 1989.

Rajneesh, Bhagwan Shree (Osho). *The Book: An Introduction to the Teachings of Bhagwan Shree Rajneesh.* Rajneeshpuram, OR: Rajneesh Foundation International, 1984.

CHAPTER 7:

Perry, John D., and Beverly Whipple. *Female Ejaculation by Grafenberg Stimulation.* A Special Presentation at the Annual Meeting of the Society for the Study of Sex, Dallas, Nov. 15, 1980.

Sevely, J. Lowndes, and J.W. Bennett. *Concerning Female Ejaculation and the Female Prostate.* The Journal of Sex Research, Feb., 1978.

Masters, William H., and Virginia E. Johnson. *Anatomy of the Female Orgasm.* The Encyclopedia of Sexual Behavior, edited by Ellis and Abarbanel, New York: 1961.

Greer, Germaine. *The Female Eunuch.* New York: McGraw-Hill, 1970.

Ladas, Alice Kahn, Beverly Whipple, and John D. Perry. *The G-Spot and Other Recent Discoveries about Human Sexuality.* New York: Holt, Rinehart and Winston, 1982.

Sundhal, Deborah. *Tantric Journey to Female Orgasm.* Santa Fe, NM: Isis Media, 1998.

Muir, Charles and Caroline. *Tantra: The Art of Conscious Loving.* San Francisco: Mercury House, 1989.

CHAPTER 8:

Masters, William H., and Virginia E. Johnson. *Human Sexual Response.* Boston: Little, Brown and Co., 1966.

Chang, Stephen T., *The Tao of Sexology: The Book of Infinite Wisdom.* San Francisco: Tao Publishing, 1986.

Anand, Margo. *The Art of Sexual Ecstasy: The Path of Sacred Sexuality for Western Lovers.* Los Angeles: Jeremy P. Tarcher, 1989.

Ramsdale, David Alan, and Ellen Jo Dorfman. *Sexual Energy Ecstasy: A Guide to the Ultimate Sexual Experience.* Playa Del Rey: Peak Skill Publishing, 1985.

Perry, John D., and Beverly Whipple. *If Your Sexual Response is Poor, the Cause Could Be Weak PC Muscles.* Forum: The International Journal of Human Relations, 1981.

Chia, Mantak. *Taoist Secrets of Love: Cultivating Male Sexual Energy.* New York: Aurora Press, 1984.

Muir, Charles and Caroline. *Tantra: The Art of Conscious Loving.* San Francisco: Mercury House, 1989.

CHAPTER 9:

Reich, Wilhelm. *The Function of Orgasm.* Translated by Vincent R. Carfagno, New York: Farrar, Straus and Giroux, 1973.

Saraswati, Sunyata, and Bodhi Avinasha. *Jewel in the Lotus: The Sexual Path to Higher Consciousness.* San Francisco: Kriya Jyoti Tantra Society, 1987.

Rajneesh, Bhagwan Shree (Osho). *The Book: An Introduction to the Teachings of Bhagwan Shree Rajneesh.* Rajneeshpuram, OR: Rajneesh Foundation International, 1984.

Woods, Margo. *Masturbation Tantra and Self Love.* Published by Mho and Mho Works, 1981.

Chia, Mantak. *Taoists Secrets of Love: Cultivating Male Sexual Energy.* New York: Aurora Press, 1984.

Sky, Michael. *Breathing: Expanding Your Power and Energy.* Bear and Co. Publishing, Santa Fe, NM, 1990.

CHAPTER 10:

Saraswati, Sunyata, and Bodhi Avinasha. *Jewel in the Lotus: The Sexual Path to Higher Consciousness.* San Francisco: Kriya Jyoti Tantra Society, 1987.

Muir, Charles and Caroline. *Tantra: The Art of Conscious Loving.* San Francisco: Mercury House, 1989.

Douglas, Nik. *Spiritual Sex: Secrets of Tantra From the Ice Age to the New Millennium.* New York: Pocket Books, 1997.

Anand, Margo. *The Art of Sexual Ecstasy: The Path of Sacred Sexuality for Western Lovers.* Los Angeles: Jeremy P. Tarcher, 1989.

CHAPTER 11:

Anand, Margo. *The Art of Sexual Ecstasy: The Path of Sacred Sexuality for Western Lovers.* Los Angeles: Jeremy P. Tarcher, 1989.

Chia, Mantak. *Taoists Secrets of Love: Cultivating Male Sexual Energy.* New York: Aurora Press, 1984.

Douglas, Nik. *Spiritual Sex: Secrets of Tantra From the Ice Age to the New Millennium.* New York: Pocket Books, 1997.

Ramsdale, David Alan, and Ellen Jo Dorfman. *Sexual Energy Ecstasy: A Guide to the Ultimate Sexual Experience.* Playa Del Rey: Peak Skill Publishing, 1985.

Wauters, Ambika. *The Book of Chakras.* Barron's Educational Series, New York: 2002.

CHAPTER 12:

Saraswati, Sunyata, and Bodhi Avinasha. *Jewel in the Lotus: The Sexual Path to Higher Consciousness.* San Francisco: Kriya Jyoti Tantra Society, 1987.

Woods, Margo. *Masturbation Tantra and Self Love*. Published by Mho and Mho Works, 1981.

Muir, Charles and Caroline. *Tantra: The Art of Conscious Loving*. San Francisco: Mercury House, 1989.

Sky, Michael. *Breathing: Expanding Your Power and Energy*. Bear and Co. Publishing, Santa Fe, NM 1990.

CHAPTER 13:

Muir, Charles and Caroline. *Tantra: The Art of Conscious Loving*. San Francisco: Mercury House, 1989.

Douglas, Nik. *Spiritual Sex: Secrets of Tantra From the Ice Age to the New Millennium*. New York: Pocket Books, 1997.

Anand, Margo. *The Art of Sexual Ecstasy: The Path of Sacred Sexuality for Western Lovers*. Los Angeles: Jeremy P. Tarcher, 1989.

Rajneesh, Bhagwan Shree (Osho). *The Book: An Introduction to the Teachings of Bhagwan Shree Rajneesh*. Rajneeshpuram, OR: Rajneesh Foundation Internationa

ABOUT THE AUTHOR

Victor Gold is a holistic health educator specializing in erotic spirituality. He has a private practice offering tantric instruction and sexual healing in Santa Rosa, California. Victor has been featured in several instructional videos including Deborah Sundhal's *Tantric Journey To Female Orgasm* and *Joseph Kramer's The Best of Vulva Massage*. He is the author of *The Potency Principles: Transforming Sexual Energy Into Spiritual Power*, an ebook entitled, *How To Maximize Your Sexual Pleasure*, and a groundbreaking audio course written with Aimée Lyndon-Adams, *How To Prolong Your Sexual Orgasm*.

CONNECT WITH VICTOR GOLD

Sign up for Victor's newsletter at
www.victorgold.net/free

To find out more information visit his website:
www.victorgold.net
www.howtoprolongsexualorgasm.com

Facebook:
www.facebook.com/Spiritual-Sex

Other books:
www.victorgold.net/otherbooks

BOOK DISCOUNTS AND SPECIAL DEALS

Sign up for free to get discounts and special deals on our bestselling books at
www.TCKpublishing.com/bookdeals

www.ingramcontent.com/pod-product-compliance
Lightning Source LLC
Chambersburg PA
CBHW070147080526
44586CB00015B/1883